Instructor's Manual/Test Bank

to accompany

Biays/Wershoven

Along These Lines
Writing Paragraphs and Essays
Sixth Edition

LaVonne McIver
Essex County College

Boston   Columbus   Indianapolis   New York   San Francisco   Upper Saddle River

Amsterdam   Cape Town   Dubai   London   Madrid   Milan   Munich   Paris   Montreal   Toronto

Delhi   Mexico City   São Paulo   Sydney   Hong Kong   Seoul   Singapore   Taipei   Tokyo

Instructor's Manual/Test Bank to accompany Biays/Wershoven, *Along These Lines: Writing Paragraphs and Essays, Sixth Edition*

Copyright ©2012, 2010, 2007, 2004 Pearson Education, Inc.

1 2 3 4 5 6 7 8 9 10—OPM—14 13 12 11

www.pearsonhighered.com

ISBN 10: 0-205-11019-3
ISBN 13: 978-0-205-11019-3

TABLE OF CONTENTS

Developmental Writing Student Supplements

Q: Would your students benefit from additional exercises that offer both practice and application of basic writing skills, with direct links to additional online practice at MyWritingLab.com?
The Pearson Lab Manual for Developing Writers (Sentences 0-205-63409-5/ Paragraphs 0-205-69341-5/
Essays: 0-205-69340-7)
This three-volume workbook is an ideal supplement for any developmental writing sequence. References direct students to Pearson's MyWritingLab, the marketing-leading online practice system, for even more practice.
- **Volume A: Sentences (0-205-63409-5)**
At this level, exercises and applications of grammar, punctuation and mechanics stress rules rather than simply skill and drill. There are many composing exercises that apply sentence skills explained in the students' primary textbook.
- **Volume B: Paragraphs (0-205-69341-5) & Volume C: Essays (0-205-69340-7)**
The exercises encourage students to apply key concepts covered in most writing classes—i.e. topic sentences, thesis statements, coherence, unity, levels of development. *Analysis* exercises give further illustration of concepts explained in class and in the primary textbook; *Building* exercises give students the "raw materials" to develop paragraphs and/or essays along the various modes. Revision prompts encourage students to look at specific key elements of their own writing and assess whether they have met the needs of their reading audience.

Q: Would your students benefit from having real student essays and quality student models?
The Pearson Student Essays Booklet (0-205-60544-3)
This brief booklet of student models includes two essays from each of the nine modes. It also includes an essay that showcases the writing process from beginning to end, crystallizing the importance of revision for all writers.

Q: Are your students visual learners? Would they benefit from exercises and writing prompts surrounding various images from everyday life, art, career, education?
Pearson Visual Writing Guide for Developing Writers by Ileen L. Linden (0-205-61984-3)
The Pearson Visual Writing Guide for Developing Writers is a thematic supplement designed to stimulate reading comprehension through an authentic perspective of visual imagery. Each assignment challenges the learner to think beyond the text to the image, expanding their worldview as they navigate through complex or unfamiliar issues. This approach teaches deconstruction, a problem-based strategy that reveals important social and cultural interrelationships across the curriculum. Instructors will find this a practical guide for assignments directed toward journaling, reflection, argumentative essay writing and more.

Q: Do you require your students to have a portfolio? Would a daily/monthly/yearly planner help them to get organized?
The Pearson Student Planner (0-205-66301-X)
This unique supplement provides students with a space to plan, think about, and present their work. In addition to the yearly planner, this portfolio includes an assessing/organizing area, daily planner for students including daily, weekly, and monthly calendars, and a useful links page.

Q: Do you require your students to keep a writing journal, and would students benefit from prompts and exercises within the journal to help guide their writing? Would a planner included directly in this journal help keep them organized through the semester?
The Pearson Writer's Journal and Student Planner by Mimi Markus (0-205-64665-4)
This supplement gives students a place to explore their own writing in the writer's journal section while also giving them space to stay organized in the student planner section. The journal portion of the supplement guides students' writing through prewriting strategies, suggested themes for their journal

writing, and sample student entries. In the planner section, students can use the monthly, weekly, and daily calendars to effectively manage their time and their course assignments.

Q: Would your students benefit from seeing how writing is relevant to a range of careers?
Applying English to Your Career by Deborah Davis (0-131-92115-0)
This supplement includes a brief page of instruction on 25 key writing skills, followed by practice exercises in these skills that focus on seven specific career fields.

Q: Would you like help in providing your students with more grammar and mechanics exercises?
Eighty Practices by Maxine Hairston Emerita (0-673-53422-7)
A collection of ten-item exercises that provide additional practice for specific grammatical usage problems, such as comma splices, capitalization, and pronouns.

The Pearson Grammar Workbook, 2/e by Jeanette Adkins (0-131-94771-0)
This workbook is a comprehensive source of instruction for students who need additional grammar, punctuation, and mechanics assistance. Covering such topics as subject-verb agreement, conjunctions, modifiers, capital letters, and vocabulary, each chapter provides helpful explanations, examples, and exercises.

The Pearson ESL Workbook, 2/e by Susan Miller and Karen Standridge (0-131-94759-1)
This workbook is divided into seven major units, each of which provides thorough explanations and exercises in the most challenging grammar topics for non-native speakers of English. Topics include nouns, articles, verbs, modifiers, pronouns, prepositions, and sentence structure.

Q: Do you have your students evaluate their peers' work? Would you like them to have an evaluation guide to help them review for their work and the work of their classmates?
What Every Student Should Know About Practicing Peer Review (0-321-44848-0)
Michelle Trim

Q: Do you have your students work in groups? Would you like them to have a guide to maximize the group work?
Learning Together: An Introduction to Collaborative Learning by Tori Haring-Smith (0-673-46848-8)
This brief guide to the fundamentals of collaborative learning teaches students how to work effectively in groups.

Q: Would you like help in providing your students with more editing exercises?
- **Print: Pearson Editing Exercises (Student / 0-205-66618-3, Instructor Answer Key / 0-205-66617-5)**
The Editing Exercises booklet contains fifty one-page editing paragraphs that provide students with opportunities to learn how to recognize and correct the most common types of sentence, grammar, and mechanical errors in context. Embedding the errors within the context of informative paragraphs rather than using discrete sentence exercises simulates a more natural writing situation, allowing students to draw upon their intuitive knowledge of structure and syntax, as well as specific information from class instruction. The booklet makes an ideal supplement to any grammar, sentence, or writing text. Various editing topics can be assigned to coordinate with class lessons, or they may be assigned individually based on problems observed in students' writing. Students may also complete selected exercises as an enrichment activity, either on their own or in collaboration with other students. Additionally, the variety of topics in the paragraphs themselves can also be used as springboards for discussion or journaling, or as models for writing assignments if desired.
- **Online: MyWritingLab APPLY exercises**
Get students reviewing and responding to students' paragraphs Go to www.mywritinglab.com for more information

Q: Would you like help in providing your students with more writing assignment topics?
100 Things to Write About Ron Koertge (0-673-98239-4)
This brief book contains over 100 individual writing assignments, on a variety of topics and in a wide range of formats, from expressive to analytical writing.

Q: Do you assign a research paper? Would students benefit from brief guides explaining specific aspects of research?
What Every Student Should Know About Researching Online (0-321-44531-7)
David Munger / Shireen Campbell

What Every Student Should Know About Citing Sources with APA Documentation (0-205-49923-6)
Chalon E. Anderson / Amy T. Carrell / Jimmy L. Widdifield, Jr.

What Every Student Should Know About Citing Sources with MLA Documentation (0-321-44737-9)
Michael Greer

What Every Student Should Know About Avoiding Plagiarism (0-321-44689-5)
Linda Stern

Q: Do you require a dictionary or stress the need of owning a dictionary?
The New American Webster Handy College Dictionary, 3/e (0-451-18166-2)
A paperback reference text with more than 100,000 entries.

Q: Do you require and/or suggest a thesaurus?
The Oxford Essential Thesaurus (0-425-16421-7)
From Oxford University Press, renowned for quality educational and reference works, comes this concise, easy-to-use thesaurus - the essential tool for finding just the right word for every occasion. The 528 page book includes 175,000 synonyms in a simple A-to-Z format, more than 10,000 entries, extensive word choices, example sentences and phrases, and guidance on usage, punctuation, and more in exclusive "Writers Toolkit."

Q: Do you require a dictionary and/or thesaurus?
The Oxford American Desk Dictionary and Thesaurus, 2/e (0-425-18068-9)
From the Oxford University Press and Berkley Publishing Group comes this one-of-a-kind reference book that combines both of the essential language tools—dictionary and thesaurus—in a single, integrated A-to-Z volume. The 1,024 page book offers more than 150,000 entries, definitions, and synonyms so you can find the right word every time, as well as appendices of valuable quick-reference information including: signs and symbols, weights and measures, presidents of the U.S., U.S. states and capitals, and more.

Penguin Discount Novel Program

In cooperation with Penguin Putnam, Inc., Pearson is proud to offer a variety of Penguin paperbacks at a significant discount when packaged with any Pearson title. Excellent additions to any English course, Penguin titles give students the opportunity to explore contemporary and classical fiction and drama. The available titles include works by authors as diverse as Toni Morrison, Julia Alvarez, Mary Shelley, and Shakespeare. To review the complete list of titles available, visit the Pearson-Penguin-Putnam website: http://www.pearsonhighered.com/penguin.

What Every Student Should Know About (WESSKA) Series

The **What Every Student Should Know About...** series is a collection of guide books designed to help students with specific topics that are important in a number of different college courses. Instructors can package any one of these booklets with their Pearson textbook for no additional charge, or the booklets can be purchased separately.

What Every Student Should Know About Preparing Effective Oral Presentations **(0-205-50545-7)**
Martin R. Cox

What Every Student Should Know About Researching Online **(0-321-44531-7)**
David Munger / Shireen Campbell

What Every Student Should Know About Citing Sources with APA Documentation **(0-205-49923-6)**
Chalon E. Anderson / Amy T. Carrell / Jimmy L. Widdifield, Jr.

What Every Student Should Know About Citing Sources with MLA Documentation **(0-321-44737-9)**
Michael Greer

What Every Student Should Know About Avoiding Plagiarism **(0-321-44689-5)**
Linda Stern

What Every Student Should Know About Practicing Peer Review **(0-321-44848-0)**
Michelle Trim

Multimedia Offerings

Q: Do your students have trouble transferring skill and drill lessons into their own writing or seeing errors in others' writing? • Would you like constant awareness of your students' progress and work in an easy-to-use tracking system? • Would a mastery results reporter help you to plan your lectures according to your class' weaknesses? • Do you want to save time by having work automatically graded and feedback supplied?
MyWritingLab (www.mywritinglab.com)
MyWritingLab is a complete online learning system with *better* practice exercises to make students better writers. The exercises in MyWritingLab are progressive, which means within each skill module students move from literal comprehension to critical application to demonstrating their skills in their own writing. The 9,000+ exercises in the system do rehearse grammar, but they also extend into the writing process, paragraph development, essay development, and research. A thorough diagnostic test outlines where student have not yet mastered the skill, and an easy-to-use tracking systems enables students and instructors to monitor all work in MyWritingLab.

STATE SPECIFIC SUPPLEMENTS

For Florida Adopters:
Thinking Through the Test: A Study Guide for the Florida College Basic Skills Exit Test, by D.J. Henry and Mimi Markus

FOR FLORIDA ADOPTIONS ONLY. This workbook helps students strengthen their reading skills in preparation for the Florida College Basic Skills Exit Test. It features both diagnostic tests to help assess areas that may need improvement and exit tests to help test skill mastery. Detailed explanatory answers have been provided for almost all of the questions. *Package item only—not available for sale.*

Available Versions:

Available Versions:	
Thinking Through the Test A Study Guide for the Florida College Basic Skills Exit Tests: Reading and Writing, without Answers 3/e	0-321-38740-6
Thinking Through the Test A Study Guide for the Florida College Basic Skills Exit Tests: Reading and Writing, with Answers, 3/e	0-321-38739-2
Thinking Through the Test A Study Guide for the Florida College Basic Skills Exit Tests: Writing, with Answers, 3/e	0-321-38741-4
Thinking Through the Test A Study Guide for the Florida College Basic Skills Exit Tests: Writing, without Answers, 3/e	0-321-38934-4

Preparing for the CLAST, 7/e (Instructor/Print 0-321-01950-4)
These two, 40-item objective tests evaluate students' readiness for the Florida CLAST exams. Strategies for teaching CLAST preparedness are included.

For Texas Adopters
The Pearson THEA Study Guide, by Jeannette Harris (Student/ 0-321-27240-4)
Created specifically for students in Texas, this study guide includes straightforward explanations and numerous practice exercises to help students prepare for the reading and writing sections of THEA Test. *Package item only—not available for sale.*

For New York/CUNY Adopters
Preparing for the CUNY-ACT Reading and Writing Test, edited by Patricia Licklider (Student/ 0-321-19608-2)
This booklet, prepared by reading and writing faculty from across the CUNY system, is designed to help students prepare for the CUNY-ACT exit test. It includes test-taking tips, reading passages, typical exam questions, and sample writing prompts to help students become familiar with each portion of the test.

Developmental Writing Instructor Resources

Pearson is pleased to offer a variety of support materials to help make teaching developmental English easier on teachers and to help students excel in their coursework. Many of our student supplements are available free or at a greatly reduced price when packaged with a Pearson writing textbook. Contact your local Pearson sales representative for more information on pricing and how to create a package.

On the Front Lines by Donna Bontatibus (0-205-81680-0)
On the Front Lines is a practical, streamlined guide designed for the instructors—new, adjunct, temporary, and even seasoned—of developmental writing at the community college. Within eight concise chapters, instructors receive realistic, easy-to-apply advice that centers on the preparation and teaching of developmental writing in a nation with over 1,000 community colleges. Instructors will be walked through the process of preparing a syllabus; structuring the classroom experience; appealing to different learning styles; teaching with technology; constructing and evaluating assignments; and conferencing with students. This accessible guide also encourages instructors to look outside the classroom--to familiarize themselves with campus resources and policies that support the classroom experience--and to look ahead for their own professional development opportunities. Given the debates on developmental

education and the importance of first-year experience initiatives to assist with student transition and retention, there is a monumental amount of weight placed on the shoulders of instructors of developmental writing. *On the Front Lines* respects the instructor's role in the developmental writing classroom and offers practical, straightforward guidance to see the instructor through the preparation of classes to the submission of final grades.

The Pearson Developmental Writing PowerPoints (0-205-75219-5)
To complement face-to-face and online courses, The Pearson Developmental Writing PowerPoint resource provides overviews on all the elements of writing an effective essay. This pedagogically sound PowerPoint guide will provide instructors and students with informative slides on writing patterns – classification, cause/effect, argument, etc. – and common grammatical errors, with questions and answers included.

The Pearson Test Bank for Developmental Writing (Print Version) by Janice Okoomian with contributions by Mimi Markus—available via the Instructor Resource Center ONLY (0-321-08486-1)
This test bank features more than 5,000 questions in all areas of writing. In addition to extensive grammar practice, the test bank covers paragraphs and essays, including such topics as the writing process and documentation. Instructors simply log on to the Instructor Resource Center (IRC) to download and print the tests of their choice.

MyTest for The Pearson Test Bank for Developmental Writing (online only) (0-205-79834-9)
This test bank features more than 5,000 questions in all areas of writing, from grammar to paragraphing through essay writing, research, and documentation. Through this instructor friendly program instructors are able to edit these questions and tests to suit their classroom needs and are also allowed more flexibility to manage assessments at any time.

Diagnostic and Editing Tests with Exercises, 9/e (0-321-41524-8)
This collection of diagnostic tests helps instructors assess students' competence in standard written English to determine placement or to gauge progress.

The Pearson Guide to Community Service-Learning in the English Classroom and Beyond by Elizabeth Kessler Rodriguez (0-321-12749-8)
Written by Elizabeth Rodriguez Kessler of the University of Houston, this monograph provides a definition and history of service-learning, as well as an overview of how service-learning can be integrated effectively into the college classroom.

Instructor Resource Center

GETTING REGISTERED

To register for the Instructor Resource Center (IRC), go to **www.pearsonhighered.com** and click **"Educators."**

1. Click **"Catalog & Instructor Resources."**

2. Request access to download digital supplements by clicking the **"New users, request Access"** link.

Follow the provided instructions. Once you have been verified as a valid Pearson instructor, an instructor code will be emailed to you. Please use this code to set up your Pearson login name and password. After you have set up your username and password, proceed to the directions below.

DOWNLOADING RESOURCES

1. Go to http://www.pearsonhighered.com/educator, sign in using your Pearson login name and password. Under **"Download Resources"** search for your book or product by either entering the author's last name or keyword.

Download Resources

Many products in our catalog have instructor resources available for download.
Here's how to access them!

1. Find your book or product in our catalog.
Enter the author's last name and a key word from the title:

[_____] **and** [_____]

[Go]

---

2. **Select your text** from the provided results.

Everything's a Text: Readings for Composition, 1/e
Melzer & Coxwell-Teague
©2011 | Longman | Paper; 592 pp | Not Yet Published
ISBN-10: 0205639542 | ISBN-13: 9780205639540

---

3. After being directed to the catalog page for your text, click the **"Instructor Resources"** link located under the **"Resources"** tab.

Clicking the "Instructor Resources" link will provide a list of all of the book-specific print and digital resources for your text below the main title. Items available for download will have a ⊞ icon.

4. Click on the **"Show Downloadable Files"** link next to the resource you want to download.

Show Downloadable Files | More Info

A pop-up box will appear showing which files you have selected to download. Once you select the files, you will be prompted to login with an Instructor Resource Center login.

5. If you have not already signed in, you will be asked to enter your login name and password, and click the **"Submit"** button.

6. Read the terms and conditions and then click the **"I accept, proceed with download"** button to begin the download process.

Instructor Resource Center File Download

This work is protected by local and international copyright laws and is provided solely for the use of instructors in teaching their courses and assessing student learning. Dissemination or sale of any part of this work (including on the World Wide Web) will destroy the integrity of the work and is not permitted. The work and materials from this site should never be made available to students except by instructors using the accompanying text in their classes. All recipients of this work are expected to abide by these restrictions and to honor the intended pedagogical purposes and the needs of other instructors who rely on these materials.

Cancel   I accept, proceed with download

7. **"Save"** the supplement file to a folder you can easily find again.

Once you are signed into the IRC, you may continue to download additional resources from our online catalog.

Please **"Sign Out"** when you are finished.

Sample Sixteen-Week Syllabus

Week 1

Class introductions. Discuss goals, objectives, and syllabus.

Diagnostic writing assignment.

Chapter 1: Writing a Paragraph

Reading Selection: Getting Carded

Week 2

Grammar Section: Chapter 15: The Simple Sentence

Chapter 2: Illustration

Reading Selection: "A Life Full of Riches"

Week 3

Illustration paragraph due

Grammar Section: Chapters 16 and 17: Coordination and Avoiding Run-On Sentences and Comma Splices

Week 4

Chapter 3: Description

Grammar Section: Chapter 18: Subordination

Chapter 31: Sentence Variety

Reading Selection: "The Colors"

Week 5

Description paragraph due

Test on Grammar Chapters 16—18

Chapter 4: Narration

Reading Selection: "The Good Father"

Week 6

Narration paragraph due

Grammar Section: Chapter 19: Avoiding Sentence Fragments

Chapter 5: Process

Reading Selection: "Breath of Life"

Week 7

Grammar Section: Chapters 20 and 21: Parallelism and Using Adjectives and Adverbs

Chapter 6: Comparison and Contrast

Reading Selection: "Honesty and Dishonesty"

Week 8

Comparison-and-Contrast paragraph due

Grammar Test on Chapters 19-21

Chapter 7: Classification

Reading Selection: "The Dog Ate My Disk, and Other Tales of Woe"

Week 9

Classification paragraph due

Mid-term evaluations. Students write a memo to the instructor describing their progress so far and goals for the remainder of the semester. Include attendance, class participation, homework completion, grammar test average, etc.

Chapter 8: Definition

Reading Selection: "Terrorism"

Week 10

Definition paragraph due

Grammar Section: Chapters 22 and 23: Problems with Modifiers and Using Verbs Correctly

Chapter 9: Cause and Effect

Reading Selection: "Say Something"

Week 11

Cause- and-Effect paragraph due

Grammar Section: Chapter 26: Verb Consistency and Case

Chapter 10: Argument

Reading Selection: "The Case for a Tax on Sodas"

Week 12

Argument paragraph due

Test: Modifiers, Using Verbs Correctly, Verb Consistency and Case

Grammar Section: Chapter 24: Subject-Verb Agreement

Week 13

Chapters 11—13 (instructor's choice of pattern): Writing an Essay and Different Essay Patterns

Grammar Test: Chapters 22, 23, 24, 26

Reading Selections: Select two: "How to Twitter," "A Brother's Murder," "Navajo Code Talkers: The Century's Best Kept Secret"

Week 14

Essay due using one of the Discussion Prompts from reading selections.

Grammar Sections: Chapters 25 and 26: Pronoun Agreement, Reference, Consistency, and Case

Chapters 12 and 13: "Different Essay Patterns"

Write a summary of or a reaction to one of the reading selections.

Week 15

Summary or reaction due

Test: Subject-Verb Agreement, Pronoun Agreement, Reference, Consistency, and Case.

Chapter 14: Using Research to Strengthen Essays

Cover sections of Chapters 27—31 (instructor's choice).

Week 16

Class evaluations

Final exam of instructor's choice: in-class essay or grammar test or both.

Sample Fourteen-Week Syllabus

Week 1

Class introductions. Discuss goals, objectives, and syllabus.

Diagnostic writing assignment.

Chapter 1: Writing a Paragraph

Reading Selection: "Getting Carded"

Week 2

Grammar Section: Chapters 15 and 16: The Simple Sentence and Coordination

Chapter 2: Illustration

Reading Selection: "A Life Full of Riches"

Week 3

Illustration paragraph due

Grammar Section: Chapters 17 and 18: Avoiding Run-On Sentences and Comma Splices, and Subordination

Chapter 3: Description

Reading Selection: "The Colors"

Week 4

Description paragraph due

Test on Grammar Chapters 15—18

Chapter 4: Narration

Reading Selection: "The Good Father"

Week 5

Narration paragraph due

Grammar Section: Chapter 19: Avoiding Sentence Fragments

Chapter 5: Process

Reading Selection: "Breath of Life"

Week 6

Process paragraph due

Grammar Section: Chapters 20 and 21: Parallelism and Using Adjectives and Adverbs

Chapter 6: Comparison-and-Contrast

Reading Selection: "Honesty and Dishonesty"

Week 7

Comparison-and-Contrast paragraph due

Grammar Section: Chapter 22: Correcting Problems with Modifiers

Mid-term evaluations. Students write a memo to the instructor describing their progress so far and goals for the remainder of the semester. Include attendance, class participation, homework completion, grammar-test average, etc.

Chapter 7: Classification

Reading Selection: "The Dog Ate My Disk, and Other Tales of Woe"

Week 8

Classification paragraph due

Test: Chapters 20—22

Grammar Section: Chapters 23 and 24: Verbs

Chapter 31: Sentence Variety

Week 9

Grammar Section: Chapters 25 and 26: Pronouns

Chapter 8: Definition

Reading Selection: "Terrorism"

Week 10

Definition paragraph due

Grammar Test: Chapters 23—26

Chapter 9: Cause and Effect

Reading Selection: "Say Something"

Week 11

Cause and Effect paragraph due

Grammar Section: Chapters 28 and 29: Spelling and Words that Look Alike/Sound Alike

Chapter 10: Argument

Reading Selections: "The Case for a Tax on Sodas"

Week 12

Argument paragraph due

Grammar Section: Chapter 30: Word Choice

Chapters 11 - 13 (instructor's choice of pattern): Writing an Essay and Different Essay Patterns

Reading Selections: Select two: "How to Twitter," "A Brother's Murder," "Navajo Code Talkers: The Century's Best Kept Secret"

Week 13

Essay due

Chapter 14: Using Research to Strengthen Essays

Grammar Section: Chapter 31: Sentence Variety

Week 14

Class evaluations

Final exam of instructor's choice: In-class essay or grammar test or both.

Sample Twelve-Week Syllabus

Week 1

Class introductions. Discuss goals, objectives, and syllabus

Diagnostic writing assignment

Chapter 1: Writing a Paragraph

Reading Selection: "Getting Carded"

Week 2

Grammar Section: Chapters 15 and 16: The Simple Sentence and Coordination

Chapter 2: Illustration

Reading Selection: "A Life Full of Riches"

Week 3

Illustration paragraph due

Grammar Section: Chapters 17 and 18: Avoiding Run-On Sentences and Comma Splices, and Subordination

Instructor's choice: Chapter 3: Description: "The Colors" or Chapter 4: Narration: "The Good Father"

Week 4

Description or Narration paragraph due

Test on Grammar Chapters 15—18

Chapter 5: Process

Grammar Section: Chapter 19: Avoiding Sentence Fragments

Reading Selection: "Breath of Life"

Week 5

Process paragraph due

Grammar Section: Chapters 20 and 21: Parallelism and Using Adjectives and Adverbs

Instructor's choice: Chapter 6: Comparison and Contrast ("Honesty and Dishonesty") or Chapter 7: Classification ("The Dog Ate My Disk, and Other Tales of Woe")

Week 6

Comparison-and-Contrast or Classification paragraph due

Grammar Section: Chapter 22: Correcting Problems with Modifiers

Midterm self-evaluation. Students write a memo to the instructor describing their progress so far and goals for the remainder of the semester. Include attendance, class participation, homework completion, grammar-test average, etc.

Week 7

Grammar Test on Chapters 19—22

Instructor's choice: Chapter 8: Definition ("Terrorism") or Chapter 9: Cause and Effect ("Say Something")

Grammar Section: Chapters 23: Using Verbs Correctly

Week 8

Definition or Cause-and-Effect paragraph due

Grammar Section: Chapter 24: Subject-Verb Agreement

Chapter 10: Argument

Reading Selection: " The Case for a Tax on Sodas"

Week 9

Argument paragraph due

Grammar Section: Chapter 25: Pronoun Agreement and Reference

Chapters 11——13 (instructor's choice of pattern): Writing an Essay and Different Essay Patterns

Week 10

Essay due

Grammar Sections: Chapters 26 and 27: Pronoun Consistency and Case and Punctuation

Grammar Test on Chapters 23—27

Week 11

Essay due

Reading Selections: Select two: "How to Twitter," "A Brother's Murder," "Navajo Code Talkers: The Century's Best-Kept Secret"

Chapter 14: Using Research to Strengthen Essays

Cover sections of Chapters 28—31 (Instructor's choice)

Week 12

Class evaluations.

Final exam of instructor's choice: in-class essay or grammar test or both

Sample Eight-Week "Express Term" Syllabus

Week 1

Class introductions. Discuss goals, objectives, and syllabus.

Chapter 1: Writing a Paragraph

Reading Selection: "Getting Carded"

Grammar Section: Chapter 15: The Simple Sentence

Chapter 2: Illustration

Reading Selection: "A Life of Riches "

Week 2

Illustration paragraph due

Grammar Section: Chapters 16–18 Coordination, Avoiding Run-On Sentences and Comma Splices, and Subordination

Chapter 3: Description

Reading Selection: "The Colors"

Chapter 31: Sentence Variety

Week 3

Description paragraph due

Test on Simple Sentences, Coordination, and Subordination

Chapter 4: Narration

Reading Selection: "The Good Father"

Narration paragraph due

Chapter 5: Process

Reading Selection: "Breath of Life"

Grammar Section: Chapter 19: Avoiding Sentence Fragments

Week 4

Process paragraph due

Chapter 6: Comparison-and-Contrast

Reading Selection: "Honesty and Dishonesty"

Comparison-and-contrast paragraph due

Grammar Section: Chapter 20—21: Parallelism, and Using Adjectives and Adverbs

Test: Fragments, Parallelism, and Using Adjectives and Adverbs

Chapter 7: Classification

Reading Selection: "The Dog Ate My Disk and other Tales of Woe"

Week 5

Classification paragraph due

Chapter 9: Definition

Reading Selection: "Terrorism"

Classification paragraph due

Chapter 10: Cause and Effect

Reading Selection: "Say Something"

Grammar Section: Chapters 22—24: Correcting Problems with Modifiers, Using Verbs Correctly, Consistency and Voice, Making Subjects and Verbs Agree

Week 6

Cause- and-Effect paragraph due

Test: Modifiers and Verbs

Chapter 10: Argument

Reading Selection: "The Case for a Tax on Sodas"

Argument paragraph due

Grammar Section: Chapter 25: Pronoun Agreement and Reference

Week 7

Chapters 11 and 12 (instructor's choice of pattern): Writing an Essay and Different Essay Patterns

Reading Selections: Select two: "How to Twitter," A Brother's Murder," "Navajo Code Talkers: The Century's Best-Kept Secret"

Grammar Sections: Chapters 26—27: Pronoun Consistency and Case and Punctuation

Test on Pronoun Agreement and Reference

Essay due

Week 8

Chapter 14: Using Research to Strengthen Essays

Cover sections of Chapters 28-31 (instructor's choice)

Chapter 13: Writing from Reading

Class evaluations

Final Exam: In-class essay or grammar test on Pronoun Consistency and Case and Punctuation and/or both

Suggested Diagnostic Paragraph Topic

You have 45 minutes to plan and write an paragraph on the topic below.

Guidelines:

- Read the assigned topic carefully to determine the instructions.
- Write only on the assigned topic.
- Spend a few moments organizing your thoughts before writing.
- Begin with a short introduction and end with a concluding statement.
- Support your ideas with examples or description.
- Read over your paper before you turn it in. Correct any mistakes you find.

Topic:

Holidays may be a positive time for families to get together for fun and food, or they may be emotionally difficult events because of financial difficulties or stress. Use specific examples to describe a holiday or vacation you have had.

Suggested Format for Midterm Self-Evaluation Memo

To: (Instructor's Name)

From: (Student's Name)

Date:

Re: Midterm Self Evaluation

Overall Evaluation

In paragraph form, describe the following:

1. Your class participation

2. Your attendance. How many times have you been absent? When you were absent, did you contact the teacher or another classmate for the assignment? Have you made up missed work?

3. Homework completion. What assignments are incomplete or missing?

4. How are you doing in this class?

5. In what areas would you like to improve? How?

Writing Process

Discuss your progress with your paragraphs/essays. Have you made a passing grade on all of them? Why or why not? What part of the writing process is easiest for you? What is the hardest part of the writing process for you? What mistakes have you made more than once in your paragraphs/essays?

Best Paragraph

What has been your best paragraph/essay so far? Why? Give examples of what you did well in that paper.

Best Aspects of This Class

What have been the most helpful aspects of this class so far? Include a discussion about the homework assignments, your textbook readings, grammar instruction, and writing instruction. What are the three most important things you have learned about writing or grammar?

Suggestions for Improvement

What suggestions do you have that would make this class more helpful for you?

Goals

What are your goals for the rest of the semester? How are you going to achieve them?

What Is Good Writing

What are three ways that writers can make their writing good?

Suggested Format for Final Evaluation

This evaluation works well with a whole group discussion as the instructor writes down student comments on an overhead or board.

1. What have we done this semester? List everything students can remember about information that was discussed in class—names of readings, types of assignments, grammar lessons, tests, etc.

2. What have you learned? This may be a particular skill that the student has learned or a method of learning the student used successfully. Be sure to include mistakes because we often learn best by making mistakes.

3. What will you do differently as a result of what you have learned? How will the information learned help the student on the job, in future classes, at home, in social situations, etc.?

CHAPTER ONE OVERVIEW

Chapter Objectives: Students will be able to (1) recognize and write clear topic sentences, (2) engage in planning and revision strategies, and (3) write a paragraph reflecting effective unity, support, and coherence.

Chapter One is an introduction to the paragraph-writing process. The first step in the writing process is **prewriting**, how to generate and develop ideas. Students learn to generate ideas by **freewriting, brainstorming,** and keeping a **journal.** Exercises on freewriting and brainstorming allow students to work individually and collaboratively.

Once the paragraph has a focus, students will learn how to create effective topic sentences and recognize and revise topic sentences that are too broad or too narrow or appear in the form of announcements.

The second step in the writing process is **planning** how to organize ideas. Students examine the topic sentence and list of details, adding details when there are not enough and eliminating ones that are not related to the topic sentence.

Next, students use **coherence** to put the details that comprise the outline into proper order. The lesson introduces the concepts of **time order, emphatic order,** and **space order.** Again, practice exercises reinforce the information covered.

The lesson continues to the third step, **drafting**, in which students create the rough draft of the paragraph. Next, students **revise** their draft by making changes in the structure, in the order of the sentences, and in the content. Then, they **edit** by making changes in the word choice, in the selection of details, in punctuation, and in the pattern and kinds of sentences. They also should include **transitions**, which are words, phrases, or sentences that link ideas. A **checklist** with key terms is included to aid in revision.

Polishing and **proofreading** are the final steps in the writing process, checking for spelling errors, punctuation errors, word choice and a concluding statement. Students give the paragraph a title if one is required by the instructor. This section of the lesson includes exercises in proofreading and the final version of an illustration paragraph.

Chapter One also introduces students to the use of the **Peer Review Form**. Students read each other's work and offer constructive criticism. Such actions will make them better writers as they learn to focus on the requirements of effective paragraph writing.

Additional Collaborative Exercise for Chapter One

1. Working in groups, have students discuss a favorite or least favorite relative. Instruct them to list characteristics that can be developed into a paragraph.

CHAPTER TWO OVERVIEW

Chapter Objectives: Students will be able to (1) distinguish between general statements and specific details, and (2) write an illustration paragraph containing a clear topic sentence and sufficient supporting details.

Chapter Two explains how to write an **illustration** paragraph. Illustration means to use specific examples to support a general point. Students practice distinguishing general statements from specific examples and adding specific statements to general statements.

Next, students learn to gather ideas, create a topic sentence, and create details for an illustration paragraph. Transitions for the paragraph are included in an Infobox. Finally, students revise and edit the essay. The final version of an illustration paragraph takes students through the revising and editing phases of paragraph writing. There are three guidelines for editing and revising paragraphs:

1) Revise a draft by combining sentences.

2) Revise a draft by adding transitions.

3) Revise a draft by adding details.

Additional Collaborative Exercises for Chapter Two

1. Working in small groups, have students provide examples from their personal experiences that support a popular maxim.

    Examples: "A stitch in time saves nine."

    "A fool and his money are soon parted."

Students can decide which examples would be best for an illustration paragraph and put them in a specific order. Groups can share examples with the rest of the class.

2. Instruct students to illustrate the hardships of attending college while holding a job, being a parent, or commuting. Most students should be able to relate to one of these situations or have an acquaintance who is experiencing these hardships.

CHAPTER THREE OVERVIEW

Chapter Objectives: Students will be able to write a descriptive paragraph that (1) supports a dominant impression, and (2) contains effective sense details.

Chapter Three provides instruction for writing a **description** paragraph. The lesson stresses the importance of using specific words and phrases. Exercises in this section involve differentiating between general and specific words and terms.

Vivid description relies upon the use of sense words: look, sound, smell, taste, and feel. An Infobox provides considerations for incorporating each sense into the writing. Exercises allow students to practice application of the senses in describing various scenes, objects, and localcs.

After freewriting, brainstorming, and journal writing, students organize ideas according to a **dominant impression**, the main idea. Students then add details to support the dominant impression. The dominant impression can also serve as the topic sentence of the paragraph. Students will group descriptive details using a logical order:

1) **Time sequence** describes grouping details using chronological order.

2) **Spatial position** describes grouping details from top to bottom and from left to right.

3) **Similar types** describe items that belong to a group.

The exercises in this section involve adding details to support a dominant impression and eliminating those that do not, creating a dominant impression from details, and putting details in proper order.

At this point, students can begin drafts. The lesson provides a checklist for revising the paragraph, a list of transitions, and exercises on recognizing transitions. A completed version of a descriptive paragraph rounds out the instruction.

Additional Collaborative Exercises for Chapter Three

1. Working in groups, have students describe a busy locale as it would appear through the eyes of a tourist/visitor from a different country or culture. Sharing descriptions with the rest of the class should stimulate discussion on effective description.

2. Have students describe the college cafeteria before, during, or just after the lunch rush.

CHAPTER FOUR OVERVIEW

Chapter Objectives: Students will be able to write a narrative paragraph that (1) has a narrow focus, (2) presents details in a clear order, and (3) uses effective transitional words and phrases.

Chapter Four discusses **narration**, telling a story. The most important aspect of narrative writing is ensuring that the narrative has a point. Since the topic sentence states the point of the narrative, related exercises cover recognizing and creating topic sentences for narrative paragraphs.

The lesson contains hints (rules) for writing the paragraph:

1) The story should be clear (provide background information if necessary).

2) The story should be interesting.

3) Details must appear in an order that is easy to follow.

4) The topic must not be too big to cover in one paragraph.

5) Students must correctly punctuate a speaker's exact words.

It can be difficult to think of a topic for the narrative; therefore, students should rely upon narrative questionnaires, freewriting, and brainstorming. Students will look for details that lead to a point.

Exercises in Chapter Four enhance students' skills in recognizing good and bad topic sentences, developing topic sentences, putting details in order, and removing irrelevant details. Vivid details enhance a narrative paragraph; therefore, the lesson provides examples to illustrate this point. Practice exercises in adding vivid details follow.

Additional help comes from a list of transitions for use in a narrative paragraph, exercises on recognizing and adding transitions, a checklist for revising a narrative paragraph, and a sample narrative paragraph.

Additional Collaborative Exercises for Chapter Four

1. Divide students into four or five groups. Create a mock scenario such as a traffic accident. Have each group create a narrative of the incident; however, each group will use a different point of view: the driver, a passenger, a bystander, or a reporter.

2. Have students create a fable. The moral can serve as the topic sentence.

CHAPTER FIVE OVERVIEW

Chapter Objectives: Students will be able to (1) recognize the difference between directional and informational process papers, and (2) write a process paragraph that contains a logical sequence, consistency in person and verb tense, and effective transitional devices.

Chapter Five focuses on writing a **process** paragraph. A process explains how to do something or how something happens.

Process paragraphs follow two forms:

1) **Directional** tells the reader how to do something.

2) **Informational** describes how something happens or is done.

Students learn to avoid mixing the two kinds of processes which results in **shifts in person**, a common error.

The instructions for writing a process paragraph consist of seven steps:

1) Choose a familiar activity.

2) Choose a topic that must follow steps in a specific order.

3) Choose a fairly small topic.

4) Write a topic sentence that makes a point about the process.

5) Include all steps.

6) Put steps in the proper order.

7) Be specific in details and steps.

Exercises in the lesson cover writing a good topic sentence, including necessary materials in a process, revising the order of steps, and listing all steps.

An Infobox provides transitions for use in a process paragraph. Checklists for revising the outline and rough draft, along with the final version of a process paragraph, serve as references.

Additional Collaborative Exercises for Chapter Five

1. Have students create a recipe process. Advise them to avoid the language of a recipe (dropping *a, an, the*). Share the recipes with the class to determine if all of the steps are clear and easy to follow.

2. Have students convert a technical process such as using a computer program or a medical process to layman's terms. Converting the process to language that can be understood by a child should be even more challenging.

CHAPTER SIX OVERVIEW

Chapter Objectives: Students will be able to (1) compare or contrast two entities, (2) demonstrate knowledge of the subject-by-subject and point-by-point patterns of exposition, and (3) write a process paragraph that incorporates appropriate transitions for a specific pattern.

Comparison (pointing out similarities) and **contrast** (pointing out differences) are the topics of Chapter Six. There are six hints for writing the paragraph:

1) Limit the topic; it should not be too big to cover in a paragraph.

2) Avoid boring, obvious choices.

3) Make a point in the topic sentence by indicating whether it is a comparison or a contrast paragraph.

4) Do not announce the outcome in the topic sentence.

5) Give the topic sentence a focus: Include the specific kind of comparison or contrast made.

6) Cover both subjects in the topic sentence. Comparison and contrast paragraphs are organized using two patterns:

1) **Subject-by-Subject pattern**—discussing all the details on one subject and then discussing all the details on the second subject in the same order.

2) **Point-by-Point pattern**—discussing each point by switching back and forth between the two subjects.

The lesson provides examples using both patterns, focusing on using the same points to compare or contrast both subjects and making sure the discussion of both subjects is balanced. Exercises aid students in adding points and details; eliminating irrelevant details.

The lesson gives much attention to transitions, as they are used extensively in both comparison and contrast paragraphs. An Infobox provides a list of transitions. Exercises on choosing appropriate transitions further prepare students to incorporate transitions into their paragraphs.

Students can use the revision checklists for the outline and rough draft to make sure they have written a well-developed paragraph. The chapter also provides final versions of comparison- and- contrast paragraphs using both subject-by-subject pattern and point-by-point pattern.

Additional Collaborative Exercises for Chapter Six

1. Working in small groups, students should compare or contrast two versions of a song, movie, or television show. It should be interesting to use topics from two different decades.

    Example: Contrast *The Beverly Hillbillies* sit com and *The Beverly Hillbillies* movie.

2. Have students compare or contrast the handling of a media event in the newspaper, on television, or in the tabloids. Example: the aftermath of Hurricane Katrina.

CHAPTER SEVEN OVERVIEW

Chapter Objectives: Students will be able to (1) determine a clear basis for classifying a topic, (2) develop at least three basis-related categories, and (3) write a classification paragraph by devising key supporting details for each category.

Chapter Seven covers writing a **classification** paragraph. To classify means to divide something into categories according to some basis. The lesson provides four hints for writing classification paragraphs:

1) Divide the subject into three or more categories.

2) Pick one basis for classification.

3) Be creative.

4) Have a reason for your classification.

Practice exercises ensure understanding of the basis for classification and creating categories that fit them.

The topic sentence for a classification paragraph can be written in two ways:

1) Mention what is being classified.

2) Indicate the basis for classification, or the categories, or both.

Exercises provide practice in finding a basis for classification; identifying what does not fit the classification; and creating topic sentences and adding details. The lesson includes checklists for revising the outline and rough draft as well as the final version of a classification paragraph.

Additional Collaborative Exercises for Chapter Seven

1. Have students work in groups to classify people according to the way they respond to a national phenomenon.

2. Have students classify professors and use teaching styles as the basis for classification.

CHAPTER EIGHT OVERVIEW

Chapter Objectives: Students will be able to (1) identify formal and personal definitions, (2) recognize abstract and concrete terms, and (3) write a definition paragraph by defining a term according to its distinguishing characteristics.

Chapter Eight provides instructions for writing **definition** paragraphs. Definition explains what a term means to the writer. There are five guidelines for writing definition paragraphs:

1) Pick a word or phrase with a personal meaning.

2) Divide topic sentences into three parts:

   a) Term

   b) Class or category

   c) Distinguishing characteristics

3) Select an appropriate class or category.

4) Express your attitude toward the term in the distinguishing characteristics.

5) Use specific and concrete examples.

Exercises provide practice in designing questions to gather details, grouping related ideas to create order, and revising examples to make them more concrete.

An Infobox contains transitions for incorporation into a definition paragraph. The lesson also provides checklists for revising the outline and rough draft. Students can refer to the sample definition paragraph for guidance.

Additional Collaborative Exercises for Chapter Eight

1. Have students work in groups to define a common slang term. Have them consider

   what the term means to different groups or cultures.

2. Have students define an American practice to a foreigner unfamiliar with the custom. Examples: spring break, crowd surfing, or line dancing.

3. Have students define a complex term in a way that makes it understandable to a young

   audience. Examples: the Internet, pollination, or liposuction.

CHAPTER NINE OVERVIEW

Chapter Objectives: Students will be able to (1) identify immediate and long-range causes and effects, (2) devise suitable topics, and (3) write a cause paragraph and an effect paragraph that incorporates appropriate transitions and details.

Chapter Nine explains **cause** (the reasons for something) and **effect** (the results of something). The lesson states four rules for writing cause or effect paragraphs:

1) Select a topic that can be handled in one paragraph:

   a) It is not too broad.

   b) It does not require research.

2) Include at least three causes or three effects in the paragraph.

3) Make causes and effects specific.

4) Write a topic sentence that indicates causes or effects. This section includes key words that signal cause or effect.

Exercises focus on recognizing good topic sentences and differentiating between cause topic sentences and effect topic sentences.

Freewriting exercises generate ideas that can be divided into causes and effects. Analyzing the two lists will help students decide which type of paragraph to write. After selecting details for each cause or effect, students can create a topic sentence. Exercises in this section provide practice in creating causes or effects for various topic sentences.

The Planning section emphasizes the order of causes or effects in the paragraph. Students will arrange them using **time order**, **emphatic order**, or **logical order**. Students practice writing topic sentences for outlines, revising the order of causes and effects, and developing an outline.

The chapter provides checklists for revising the outline and rough draft. An Infobox contains transitions for use in cause paragraphs and effect paragraphs. Additional exercises cover connecting ideas, adding details, combining sentences, and correcting a final copy. The lesson includes the final version of an effect paragraph.

Additional Collaborative Exercises for Chapter Nine

1. Have students select a well-known incident/accident and develop a list of its causes or effects. Students can analyze and group them for a paragraph.

2. Have students select a new policy, business, or product. Have them consider what caused it to come into being and what will result from it. Examples: a new college policy, a new fast-food restaurant, or a new medicine.

CHAPTER TEN OVERVIEW

Chapter Objectives: Students will be able to write an effective argument paragraph that (1) respects its targeted audience, and (2) acknowledges opposing viewpoints.

Writing an **argument** paragraph is the focus of Chapter Ten. The purpose of argument is to persuade a reader to think or act in a certain way. The lesson offers five rules for writing an argument paragraph:

1) Select a topic that is small enough to handle in one paragraph.

2) Pick a topic that you understand from personal experience or observation.

3) The topic sentence should contain two elements:

    a) Name the subject of the argument.

    b) Take a stand.

4) Consider the audience's response to the argument:

    a) Refute objections.

    b) Concede a point.

    c) Turn an objection into an advantage.

5) Use reasons that are specific, clear, and logical:

    a) Use at least three reasons to support your stand.

    b) Make sure reasons do not overlap.

    c) Avoid circular argument.

Exercises in this section cover recognizing good topic sentences as well as recognizing and handling objections.

Focusing on possible objections will lead students to reasons that support the argument. After they create three reasons and supportive details, the topic sentence can be drafted. Exercises in the chapter focus on distinguishing between reasons and details and finding reasons to support an argument.

It is best to group details using emphatic order, saving the best for last. There are related exercises in the chapter in which students select the most significant reasons from lists, recognize reasons that overlap, and identify reasons that are not specific. An additional exercise involves adding details to an outline. This lesson includes a checklist for revising an argument outline.

The Drafting and Revising section provides a checklist for revising the rough draft of the paragraph. This section emphasizes the importance of covering all serious or obvious reasons in an argument. In argument, another way to convince readers is to explain the seriousness of a problem. This section also presents a list of transitions for use in the paragraph and the final version of an argument paragraph. Exercises include adding explanations, recognizing transitions, adding a final sentence, and proofreading the final version.

Additional Collaborative Exercises for Chapter Ten

1. Divide students into two groups. Have one group of students create an argument for a change that needs to be made at the college or in town. Have the other group of students take the opposing view.

2. Have students devise a new approach to eliminate a prominent social problem. Examples: illiteracy, homelessness, teen pregnancy, or DUI.

CHAPTER ELEVEN OVERVIEW

Chapter Objectives: Students will be able to (1) identify the basic components of an essay, (2) recognize the differences between a topic sentence and a thesis statement, and (3) write a multi-paragraph essay containing sufficient supporting details and effective transitions.

Chapter Eleven moves beyond paragraph writing to the **essay**. The lesson begins by comparing a single paragraph and an essay to illustrate similarities; each has a main point and supports it with subpoints. The essay is divided into three parts: introduction, body, and conclusion.

The **thesis,** the main idea of the essay, goes in the introduction. The lesson provides characteristics of the thesis:

1) The thesis is expressed in a sentence. It is not the same as the topic or the title.

2) A thesis does not announce; it makes a point about the subject.

3) A thesis is not too broad.

4) A thesis is not too narrow.

Hints for writing a thesis include:

1) The thesis can mention the specific subpoints.

2) The thesis can make a point without listing the subpoints.

Exercises provide practice in recognizing good thesis statements and writing the two types of theses.

Students must narrow the topic of the essay just as they did with the single paragraphs. Freewriting, listing or clustering ideas help with this process. The lesson provides exercises in narrowing topics and clustering related ideas.

The next step is creating the outline. The **formal outline**, one that uses Roman numerals and capital letters, is one way to organize paragraphs and supporting details. The chapter provides three hints for writing the outline:

1) Check topic sentences: Each topic sentence must support the thesis, or the essay will lose its focus.

2) Include enough details: It is best to create details in the outline phase rather than during the writing phase. Writers who become rushed or run out of ideas may end up with short, sketchy paragraphs.

3) Stay on one point: Make sure that the details listed in the outline support the thesis statement. If they do not, eliminate the details that do not fit or rewrite the thesis statement.

A checklist contains considerations for revising the outline. Exercises in this section focus on adding details to an outline and writing topic sentences to support details.

The Drafting section returns to the three parts of the essay, beginning with the introduction. The thesis statement is generally positioned as the last sentence of the introductory paragraph. Six rules provide help in writing the introduction:

1) Begin with general statements.

2) Begin with a quotation.

3) Tell a story.

4) Explain about why the topic is worth writing.

5) Ask rhetorical questions.

6) Open with a contradiction of the main point.

A practice exercise lists five thesis statements. Students select one and write an introduction.

The second part of the essay is the body. This section of the chapter contains two checklists pertaining to topic sentences and body paragraphs. Exercises provide additional practice in creating topic sentences from the thesis.

The last part of the essay is the conclusion. The lesson provides three rules for writing the conclusion:

1) Restate the thesis; make the same point with different words.

2) You can make a judgment, valuation, or recommendation in the conclusion.

3) You can conclude by **framing** the essay; you take an example, question, or quotation from the introduction and refer to it in the conclusion.

Exercises in this section give practice in restating the thesis.

The chapter provides three checklists: (1) Revising an outline of the essay, (2) Developing body paragraphs of the essay (3) The topic sentence of the essay. An Infobox includes a list of transitions to use when linking paragraphs. Two ways to link paragraphs are to restate an idea or to use synonyms or repetition. Additional exercises cover identifying main points, adding transitions, and recognizing synonyms and repetition.

Final instructions cover giving the essay a title. The final version of an essay and an exercise in proofreading complete the instruction.

Additional Collaborative Exercises for Chapter Eleven

1. Divide students into pairs. Have them interview each other. Each student will consider his or her partner's goals, likes, dislikes, and opinions on specific issues. Have each student formulate a thesis about his or her partner, organize the ideas, and write a short essay.

2. Provide students with magazine or newspaper articles. Have them identify the salient features of an essay: thesis statement, topic sentences, transitions, etc.

CHAPTER TWELVE OVERVIEW

Chapter Objective: Students will be able to apply the stages of the writing process and the basic essay format to a variety of rhetorical patterns.

Building on the paragraph patterns in the previous chapters, Chapter Twelve explains how to use the same patterns to create essays:

Illustration: Use specific examples to support a general statement and develop them well.

Description: Use specific details and decide on a clear order.

Narration: Give the essay a point and divide the narrative into clear stages.

Process: Create a directional process or an informational process, divide the steps into paragraphs, and explain each step thoroughly using details.

Comparison or Contrast: Use points of comparison or contrast to organize body paragraphs and use a point-by-point pattern.

Each section explains how to gather ideas, devise a plan, add details, revise, and edit the paragraph. Each section is complete with a sample essay and writing prompts.

Additional Collaborative Exercises for Chapter Twelve

1. Provide students with a general topic. Have them develop it into two separate topic sentences for two writing patterns and create the essays.

   Examples: politics, the Internet.

2. Have students create a combined pattern essay. For example, compare and contrast two items and then argue which of the two is best.

   Examples: two boy bands, two movies, two restaurants.

CHAPTER THIRTEEN OVERVIEW

Chapter Objective: Students will be able to (1) gain further practice in applying the stages of the writing process to various rhetorical patterns and (2) recognize the flexibility of the multi-pattern essay.

Building on the paragraph patterns in the previous chapters, Chapter Thirteen further explains how to use the same patterns to create essays:

Classification: Select a topic and pick a basis for classification.

Definition: Write a personal definition, not a dictionary definition.

Cause or Effect: Choose either cause or effect and use each cause or effect as a body paragraph.

Argument: Select a topic based on personal experience, take a stand in the thesis, use the reasons in the argument to focus the body paragraphs, and consider the audience's objections.

Multi-Pattern: Start with a topic, not with a concern about the patterns. You do not shift patterns within a paragraph, and your thesis does not have to include a reference to each pattern you are using.

Each section explains how to gather ideas, devise a plan, add details, revise, and edit the paragraph. Each section is complete with a sample essay and writing prompts.

Additional Collaborative Exercises for Chapter Thirteen

1. Provide students with a topic. Have them write a thesis statement for a multi-pattern essay.

   Examples: My favorite vacation, a family tradition

2. Provide students with a controversial topic. Divide students into groups and provide each group with a position it must defend regarding the topic. Have students debate their positions.

CHAPTER FOURTEEN OVERVIEW

Chapter Objectives: Students will be able to strengthen their essays by (1) incorporating supporting details from valid sources, (2) using proper MLA documentation for internal citation and Works Cited entries, and (3) blending direct quotations and effective paraphrasing.

Chapter Fourteen discusses the research process, beginning with research in daily life and using research to strengthen essays. An example of an essay without research is given. Next, there are suggestions of how to locate material in the college library using:

1) The online catalog

2) Popular periodical indexes

3) Internet search engines

Suggestions for ways to check sources for accuracy and validity are mentioned.

The next section examines how to incorporate and acknowledge sources:

1) Gathering and organizing sources

2) Taking notes and acknowledging your sources

3) Avoiding plagiarism

4) Options for acknowledging sources

5) Signal phrases

6) Documenting information from a source with an unknown author

7) Works Cited entries

    a) Books

    b) Periodicals

    c) Electronic sources

    d) Non-print

8) Incorporating research into an outline

The final section demonstrates how the original essay without research is strengthened by using material from outside sources.

Many college assignments or tests ask students to write about an assigned reading. "Writing from Reading" is discussed in Chapter Thirteen. Students can write from reading by reacting to the reading, agreeing or disagreeing. The reading process evolves in three steps:

1) Preread: Prereading entails scanning the reading for length, subheadings, charts, graphs, illustrations, introductory material on the author or the subject, the title, and parts underlined, italicized, or emphasized in some way. Prereading helps the reader focus and allows him or her to form questions about the writing.

This section includes the article, "A Ridiculous Addiction," for students to preread. Following this are a list of items the students should have noticed while prereading and a list of possible questions that may have arisen.

2) Reading: When reading for the first time, students do so with questions in mind to get a sense of the whole piece. They should look up unfamiliar words in a dictionary or try to determine the meaning based upon context. Reading speed depends on the type of material being read.

Next, students read "A Ridiculous Addiction."

3) Rereading: Rereading involves *thinking on paper while reading* with a pen or a pencil. While rereading, students should mark main points, define words, create questions, make comments, evaluate ideas, etc. It is up to the reader how he or she will write comments or highlight points. This section shows what "A Ridiculous Addiction" might look like after a reader marks it. An exercise on reading and making notes concludes this section of the lesson.

After the reading process is completed, students can write a **summary** which states important ideas in a brief form including the writer's main idea, ideas used to explain the main idea, and examples to support the ideas. Exercises assist students in recognizing the main idea of writing for a summary.

Students must remember to attribute the ideas to the writer. The summary must contain the name of the author and the title of the selection being summarized. The lesson includes a draft of a summary followed by a discussion of the noticeable errors it contains. The final version highlights the corrections of these errors.

Instructors may require students to write their reactions to readings. Students can generate ideas by freewriting and brainstorming. Points of agreement or disagreement may arise during the reading process. Students can select one to focus on in the reaction paper. This section of the lesson includes the final version of a reaction paper.

The final discussion in Chapter Thirteen covers steps for writing an essay test:

1) Before the test: Days before the test, students should apply the steps of reading. They will review the marked assignment shortly before the test.

2) During the test: Students should follow the steps of writing. Organizing time is important to avoid problems such as writer's block, writing in circles, or omitting main ideas.

Additional Collaborative Exercise for Chapter Fourteen

1. Give groups of students an article and have them apply the reading process. You may choose from the essays in the textbook. Have them compare the items that they noticed during prereading and the items they marked during the rereading phase. A discussion follows.

CHAPTER FIFTEEN OVERVIEW

Chapter Objectives: Students will be able to (1) identify subjects and verbs in both simple sentences and in ones with complicated word order, (2) recognize helping verbs, prepositional phrases, and infinitives, and (3) correct errors in faulty sentence construction.

Chapter Fifteen analyzes the makeup of a sentence. The primary focus is on subjects and verbs, the basic parts of a sentence. Following this is instruction on prepositions and prepositional phrases, word order, and verb forms that cannot serve as main verbs. These sentence components often hinder students' efforts to recognize and create grammatically correct sentences.

There are two categories of verbs: **action verbs** and **being verbs**. Each may be used in conjunction with **helping verbs**. The lesson includes a list of frequently used helping verbs along with exercises on combining action and being verbs with helping verbs.

Once students learn verb recognition, it should not be difficult to find the subject of the sentence. Students do so by creating a question, "Who or what does the action or expresses the state of being?" The answer to the question is the subject of the sentence.

The focus now turns to prepositions and prepositional phrases. Eliminating prepositional phrases from the sentence prevents confusing parts of them with the subject of the sentence. The lesson provides a chart of common prepositions along with clues for recognizing them.

Prepositional phrases are one sentence component that have an effect on word order. In most sentences, the subject precedes the verb; beginning a sentence with a prepositional phrase reverses this order. Sentences that begin with *There is/There are, There was/There were, Here is/Here are,* or *Here was/Here were,* and questions have the same effect on word order. Exercises offer additional practice in subject and verb selection with complicated word order.

The lesson cautions students about words that resemble verbs in a sentence but are actually adverbs, such as *always, often, nearly,* etc. **Infinitives**, or **-ing verbs** cannot serve as main verbs in a sentence. These forms must be combined with a main verb or a helping verb. Practice exercises allow students to recognize and correct these types of errors.

CHAPTER SIXTEEN OVERVIEW

Chapter Objectives: Students will be able to identify and apply sentence-combining techniques that rely on coordinating conjunctions and conjunctive adverbs.

In Chapter Sixteen, students learn to combine simple sentences (independent clauses) using **coordination**. Coordination consists of three options:

Option 1: Using a comma and a **coordinating conjunction**

, for	, or
, and	, yet
, nor	, so
, but	

Two exercises on recognizing **compound sentences** (a sentence composed of two or more independent clauses) and adding commas provide additional practice.

Option 2: Using a semicolon

A semicolon can combine two simple sentences that are related in their ideas.

Option 3: Using a semicolon and a **conjunctive adverb**

An Infobox lists common conjunctive adverbs. The lesson explains when a comma is needed after the conjunctive adverb and when it is not needed:

1) A comma follows a conjunctive adverb if the conjunctive adverb is more than one syllable long.

2) A comma does not follow one-syllable conjunctive adverbs.

Chapter Fifteen concludes with exercises in combining independent clauses using all three options.

CHAPTER SEVENTEEN OVERVIEW

Chapter Objectives: Students will be able to recognize and correct run-on sentences and comma splices.

Chapter Seventeen teaches students to avoid **run-on sentences** and **comma splices**. Run-on sentences, also called fused sentences, are independent clauses that are run together. Two independent clauses can be joined with a comma and a coordinating conjunction or by a semicolon. A comma splice occurs when two independent clauses are combined using only a comma. To correct the error, use a comma and a coordinating conjunction or a semicolon. The chapter provides numerous exercises on correcting run-on sentences and comma-splice errors, including a paragraph with errors to correct.

CHAPTER EIGHTEEN OVERVIEW

Chapter Objectives: Students will be able to (1) identify sentence-combining techniques that rely on subordinating conjunctions, (2) distinguish between dependent and independent clauses, and (3) generate and punctuate sentences.

This chapter continues the discussion that begins in Chapters Sixteen and Seventeen on combining simple sentences (independent clauses). Chapter Eighteen provides two more options for combining sentences using **subordination**.

Option 4: Using a dependent clause to begin a sentence

Option 5: Using a dependent clause to end a sentence

Subordination turns independent clauses into **dependent clauses** (contains a subject and verb but does not make sense by itself) by adding a **subordinating conjunction**.

After discussing the use of subordinating conjunctions in detail, the lesson provides an Infobox that lists common subordinating conjunctions. Much emphasis is placed on punctuating **complex sentences** (a sentence with one independent clause and one or more dependent clauses). A practice exercise follows.

After thorough discussion of the two new options, the chapter reviews all five options. The exercises entail using all five options to combine simple sentences. Students also practice creating their own compound and complex sentences.

CHAPTER NINETEEN OVERVIEW

Chapter Objectives: Students will be able to recognize and correct sentence fragments.

Chapter Nineteen teaches students to recognize and avoid **sentence fragments**. This relies upon the application of two key steps:

1) Check for a subject and a verb. If the group of words lacks the subject or the verb or both, add the missing part(s).

The lesson contains two exercises on checking groups of words for subjects and verbs.

2) If there is a subject and a verb, make sure there is a complete statement. If there is no complete statement, there are several options available to fix this type of fragment:

   a) Turn the dependent clause into an independent clause by removing the subordinating conjunction.

   b) Add an independent clause to the dependent clause.

   c) Link the fragment to the sentence before or after it.

Exercises in this section focus on checking for dependent-clause fragments.

Additional exercises provide practice using both steps to recognize sentence fragments and correct them.

CHAPTER TWENTY OVERVIEW

Chapter Objectives: Students will be able to recognize parallel structure and use it to revise aswkwardly worded sentences.

The focus of Chapter Twenty is **parallelism**, giving related ideas, examples, or details a similar structure in a sentence. To ensure that sentences have parallel structure, students learn to apply two steps:

1) Look for the list in the sentence.

2) Give the parts of the list a similar structure by changing or adding words.

Exercises allow students to practice skills by revising nonparallel sentences, creating parallel lists, writing parallel sentences, and combining simple sentences.

CHAPTER TWENTY-ONE OVERVIEW

Chapter Objectives: Students will be able to identify adjectives and adverbs and incorporate them correctly in their writing.

Chapter Twenty-One focuses on the correct use of **adjectives** and **adverbs**. The lesson discusses each group individually and then collectively since students often misuse them, substituting adjectives for adverbs and vice versa.

The chapter begins by defining adjectives and providing examples. Examples of adjective placement in sentences follow. The next section discusses the **comparative form** (comparing two persons or things) and the **superlative form** (comparing three or more persons or things). Exercises in selecting the correct adjective form and creating sentences that contain adjectives reinforce the lesson.

The second half of the chapter addresses adverb use. The lesson provides a definition along with examples. Exercises entail recognizing adverbs in sentences and writing sentences that contain adverbs.

The next section provides hints to avoid misuse of adjectives and adverbs:

1) Changing adjectives to adverbs by adding the suffix, *-ly*

2) Correct use of *good* and *well*, and *bad* and *badly*

3) Avoiding the use of *more* with *-er* endings and *most* with *-est* endings

4) Correct use of *than* and *then* in comparisons

5) Correct use of commas between adjectives

To aid students in the recognition of adjective and adverb errors, the chapter provides a sample paragraph which contains common errors.

CHAPTER TWENTY-TWO OVERVIEW

Chapter Objectives: Students will be able to identify modifiers within sentences and correct misplaced or dangling modifiers.

Correcting problems with **modifiers** (words, phrases, or clauses that describe something in a sentence) is the topic of Chapter Twenty-Two. The lesson provides examples of modifiers and an exercise to ensure understanding. The instruction highlights two types of modifier problems:

1) **Misplaced modifiers**—those positioned in the sentence where it is unclear what is being modified.

2) **Dangling modifiers**—those that have nothing to modify in the sentence.

Exercises follow each discussion. Infoboxes within the chapter serve as quick references for the steps of recognizing and correcting modifier problems.

CHAPTER TWENTY-THREE OVERVIEW

Chapter Objectives: Students will be able to (1) identify standard and irregular verb forms, (2) recognize errors in verb tense or consistency, and (3) distinguish between passive and active voice.

The purpose of Chapter Twenty-Three is to teach students to speak and write effectively using standard English forms. The lesson focuses on verb forms: **past tense**, **present** and **past participle**, and **irregular verb** usage.

The section on past and present tenses presents the forms in first, second, and third person (singular and plural). Exercises involve selecting the correct verb forms in past and present tenses for sentences.

Next, the lesson introduces students to the present participle (the -*ing* form used with helping verbs) and past participle (the form used with *have*, *has*, or *had*). The instruction details the formation of present and past participles.

The majority of the section on irregular verbs focuses on the correct usage of *be*, *have*, and *do*. The exercises provide practice in using the three verbs correctly when indicating past or present tense. Although the primary focus is on *be*, *have*, and *do*, the lesson does, however, provide a lengthy list of irregular verbs that includes present, past, and past participle forms. Exercises that incorporate irregular verbs from the list conclude the lesson.

CHAPTER TWENTY-FOUR OVERVIEW

Chapter Objectives: Students will be able to (1) identify correct subject-verb agreement and (2) recognize prepositional phrases, compound subjects, indefinite pronouns, and collective nouns.

Chapter Twenty-Four covers **consistency of verb tense** and **voice**, introduces two more tenses (**present perfect** and **past perfect**), and explains **active** and **passive voice**.

The lesson begins with consistency of verb tense, staying in one tense. Students practice correcting sentences and paragraphs with errors in tense.

The next section explains the additional tenses:

1) Present perfect tense—the past participle of a verb plus *have* or *has*. The present perfect tense shows an action that began in the past and is still going on in the present.

2) Past perfect tense—the past participle form of the verb plus *had*. Past perfect tense shows when two or more things happened at different times in the past.

Exercises allow students to differentiate between past tense and present perfect/past perfect tenses.

The final exercises in this lesson focus on voice:

1) Active voice—the subject in the sentence performs the action.

2) Passive voice—the subject receives the action of the verb.

Students learn to avoid unnecessary shifts in voice. Practice exercises entail rewriting sentences by changing passive voice to active voice and correcting shifts in voice.

Additional hints on verb use cover common errors such as using *use to* instead of *used to*, using *should of, could of,* and *would of* instead of *should have, could have,* and *would have,* and using *would have* when *had* is the correct choice. A comprehensive exercise covering all areas of instruction concludes the lesson.

CHAPTER TWENTY-FIVE OVERVIEW

Chapter Objectives: Students will be able to (1) identify pronoun antecedents, indefinite pronouns, and collective nouns, and (2) correct errors in pronoun agreement and reference.

Chapter Twenty-Five covers the rules of subject-verb agreement. Subjects (nouns and pronouns) and verbs must agree in number. The lesson discusses specific problems and considerations concerning agreement:

1) Prepositional phrases: The objects of prepositions cannot be part of the subject.

2) Changed word order: The subject does not come before the verb in the sentence.

3) Compound subjects:

   a) When two or more subjects are joined by *and*, use a plural verb.

   b) When two or more subjects are joined by *or, either. . .or, neither. . .nor,* or

   not only. . .but also, the verb agrees with the subject closer to the verb.

4) Indefinite pronouns: Indefinite pronouns take singular verbs. The chapter includes a list of indefinite pronouns.

5) Collective nouns: Collective nouns take singular verbs unless the members of the group are acting individually. Then a plural verb is used.

Exercises cover each section individually and collectively.

CHAPTER TWENTY-SIX OVERVIEW

Chapter Objectives: Students will be able to (1) recognize first-, second-, and third-person points of view, (2) correct errors in pronoun inconsistency, and (3) use appropriate pronoun cases in their writing.

Chapter Twenty-Six focuses on points of view and pronoun consistency, common errors with case of pronouns, and choosing the case of pronouns

The chapter gives examples of common mistakes along with methods to correct them. Practice exercises in rewriting sentences for clear pronoun reference conclude the lesson.

CHAPTER TWENTY-SEVEN OVERVIEW

Chapter Objectives: Students will be able to demonstrate proficiency in basic punctuation skills, including (but not limited to) the proper use of commas, semicolons, colons, apostrophes, parentheses, numbers, capital letters, and abbreviations.

This chapter begins a review of the basic rules of punctuation. Chapter Twenty-Seven discusses the use of the **period** and the **question mark**.
The period is used to mark the end of a sentence that makes a statement and after abbreviations. The question mark is used after a direct question. Exercises on punctuating with periods and question marks follow the discussion.

Chapter Twenty-Seven explains the four main ways to use the **comma**: lister, linker, introducer, and inserter. Next, there is a discussion of the minor uses of the comma: with quotations, with dates and addresses, in numbers, and for clarity.

In addition, Chapter Twenty-Seven reviews the uses of the **semicolon** and **colon**. Use a semicolon to join two independent clauses and to separate items on a list that contains commas. The colon is used at the end of a complete statement to introduce a list or explanation and to introduce long quotations. Exercises on punctuating with semicolons and colons follow the lesson.

Chapter Twenty-Seven also explains how to use the **apostrophe** in contractions, to show possession, for special uses of time, and to create a plural of numbers mentioned as numbers, letters mentioned as letters, and words that normally do not have plurals. Practice exercises complete the lesson.

CHAPTER TWENTY-EIGHT OVERVIEW

Chapter Objectives: Students will be able to (1) distinguish between vowels and consonants, (2) apply basic spelling rules to determine proper word endings and variations, and (3) recognize when a one- or two-word spelling applies to certain terms.

Chapter Twenty-Eight discusses rules for spelling. First, the lesson explains the difference between **vowels** and **consonants** in order for students to fully understand the spelling rules. Five rules are emphasized:

1) Doubling a final consonant

2) Dropping the final *e*

3) Changing the final *y* to *i*

4) Adding *-s* or *-es*

5) Using *ie* or *ei*

Practice exercises appear after each discussion. There is also a comprehensive exercise and a paragraph that students edit for spelling errors.

The next section of the lesson addresses words that should or should not be combined to make one word and words whose spelling depends on their meaning. Students practice by selecting the correct word(s) in sentences and a paragraph. An extensive list of commonly misspelled words completes the lesson.

CHAPTER TWENTY-NINE OVERVIEW

Chapter Objectives: Students will be able to distinguish between common sound-alike and look-alike words and incorporate such distinctions in their writing.

Chapter Twenty-Nine provides an extensive list of words that sound alike or look alike. Each grouping gives a definition of each word and incorporates each word into a sentence. Exercises appear at intervals in the alphabetized list of words. The breaks allow students to become familiar with small groups of words before moving on to new ones.

Students practice selecting the correct word in sentences, creating sentences, and editing paragraphs for words that sound alike or look alike.

CHAPTER THIRTY OVERVIEW

Chapter Objectives: Students will be able to (1) identify examples of wordiness, slang, and clichés and (2) gain an appreciation for precise word choice (diction) in their writing.

Students can improve their writing by paying close attention to **word choice**, the topic of Chapter Thirty-Four. The discussion advises students to avoid **general language**, **wordiness**, and **clichés**:

1) General language: Use precise language to replace vague, general words and phrases.

2) Wordiness: Be precise and direct: avoid the use of extra, unnecessary words.

3) Clichés: Avoid clichés as ways of making a point; they are old and no longer clever.

Related exercises allow students to revise sentences by using precise language, eliminating wordiness, and replacing clichés with thoughtful words or phrases.

CHAPTER THIRTY-ONE OVERVIEW

Chapter Objectives: Students will be able to recognize a variety of sentence patterns and incorporate an effective balance of long and short sentences in their writing.

The focus of Chapter Thirty-Five is **sentence variety**, using different lengths and types of sentences. Students learn to balance long and short sentences; begin sentences differently (change the word order); use-*ing* **modifiers;** use **appositives**; and use *who*, *which*, or *that*, and *-ed* **clauses**:

1) Balancing long and short sentences: Avoid paragraphs filled only with short, choppy sentences or long, complicated ones.

The lesson includes paragraphs filled only with short or long sentences. Revised paragraphs follow each sample. Exercises give students practice in combining short sentences and shortening long ones in paragraphs that are not balanced.

2) Beginning sentences differently: To break monotony, change word order by beginning some sentences with adverbs and prepositional phrases.

Students practice adding both to sentences in practice exercises.

3) Combine sentences using *-ing* or *-ed* modifiers: These two methods turn one of the sentences into a phrase.

In practice exercises, students combine pairs of sentences using both modifiers.

4) Using appositives (a word or phrase that renames or describes a noun): An appositive can be inserted at the beginning, middle, or end of a sentence.

As in the previous exercise, students combine pairs of sentences for practice.

5) Using *who*, *which*, or *that* clauses: Using these clauses provides other methods to combine short, choppy sentences. After combining sentences, students must decide if the clauses contain essential or nonessential information and punctuate them accordingly.

Related exercises follow the discussion along with a comprehensive exercise.

APPENDIX: READING FOR WRITERS

Many college assignments or tests ask students to write about an assigned reading. "Writing from Reading" is discussed in the appendix. Students can write from reading by reacting to the reading, agreeing or disagreeing. The reading process evolves in three steps:

1) Preread: Prereading entails scanning the reading for length, subheadings, charts, graphs, illustrations, introductory material on the author or the subject, the title, and parts underlined, italicized, or emphasized in some way. Prereading helps the reader focus and allows him or her to form questions about the writing.

2) Read: When reading for the first time, students do so with questions in mind to get a sense of the whole piece. They should look up unfamiliar words in a dictionary or try to determine the meanings based upon context. Reading speed depends on the type of material being read.

3) Reread: Rereading involves *thinking on paper while reading* with a pen or a pencil. While rereading, students should mark main points, define words, create questions, make comments, evaluate ideas, etc. It is up to the reader how he or she will write comments or highlight points. This section shows what "A Ridiculous Addiction" might look like after a reader marks it. An exercise on reading and making notes concludes this section of the lesson.

This section includes the article, "Manners Matter Online" for students to re-read. Following the article is a sample summary. The Role of Critical thinking; Developing Points of Agreement; and Writing on a Related Idea conclude this section.

Reading selections conclude the Appendix:

Reading Summaries:

Readings for Writers: "Manners Matter Online: Basic Etiquette Applies Even for E-Mail," by Amritha Alladi

Alladi wrote this article for the Gainesville (Florida) Sun, and she focuses on why students and other young people seeking employment need to sharpen their e-mail communication skills.

Readings for Writers: The Writing Process, "Getting Carded" by David Migoya

The essay explores a rite of passage for most Americans: getting their first credit card. The author warns that the card, a symbol of maturity, has its dangers.

Readings for Writers: Illustration, "A Life Full of Riches," by Karl R. Green

Karl R. Green lives in Cedar Rapids, Iowa. In this essay, originally published in Newsweek in 2007, Green gives many examples of the "riches" he enjoys. He notes, "This material world constantly reminds me of what I don't have. But somehow I still feel wealthy."

Readings for Writers: Description, "The Colors," by Gary Soto

In this essay, Gary Soto describes his childhood world of Fresno, California. The Mexican-American poet, essayist, and short story writer relies heavily on the senses of sight, smell, sound, and touch as he writes of the summer days at his grandparents' house.

Readings for Writers: Narration, "The Good Father," by Alisa Valdes-Rodriguez

After overcoming a tumultuous childhood himself, the author's father becomes both mother and father to his own children. She thanks him with this essay which tells the story of her Cuban-born father.

Readings for Writers: Process, "Breath of Life" by Judith Sachs

After asserting that you can turn breathing into a meaningful twenty-minute activity that will help you get a deeper sense of yourself, Sachs describes the process of "creative breathing." In this essay, Sachs demonstrates how you can take a vacation from stress by performing the "Breath of Life" exercise, the process of which she describes in the essay.

Readings for Writers: Comparison or Contrast, "Honesty and Dishonesty" by Jo-Allen Dimitirus and Mark Mazzarella

This essay compares and contrasts the different kinds of liars, and it outlines the physical clues that occur when a person lies. The authors assert that honest people are relaxed and open in contrast to dishonest people, who are not.

Readings for Writers: Classification, "The Dog Ate My Disk, and Other Tales of Woe," by Carolyn Foster Segal

Carolyn Foster Segal originally wrote this article for *The Chronicle of Higher Education*, a magazine for college teachers. An English professor, Segal classifies student excuses according to the kind of misfortune they describe. Note that this essay was written for college teachers and see if you, as a student, find it amusing.

Readings for Writers: Definition, "Terrorism," by Ron Cunningham

Ron Cunningham is the editorial-page editor of the Gainesville (Florida) Sun. In this 2010 editorial, he defines terrorism in two ways: (1) as the national fear of flying, bombing, and other attacks by enemies abroad, and (2) as a fear that we ignore each time we drive. As he notes, "In a typical month, more of us are killed in traffic than perished in the attacks of 9–11." Consider whether his definitions make too little of global terrorism or make the reader think about highway safety.

Readings for Writers: Cause and Effect, "Say Something," by Lucie Prinz

Lucie Prinz writes about some adults' fear of teenagers and explains the effects of that fear. She uses two incidents, both of which take place on a subway, to ask why these adults are reluctant to interact with "the ordinary, harmless children we all come in contact with every day."

Readings for Writers: Argument, "The Case for a Tax on Sodas," by Jo Ivey Boufford

Boufford, president of the New York Academy of Medicine, writes about a growing concern in this country: the role of sugary drinks in the obesity epidemic. The statistics and studies in her article, published in 2010, are used to argue that a tax on sodas (combined with other programs and policies) could save lives.

Readings for Writers: The Essay, "How to Twitter," by Julia Angwin

Writing widely on issues of media and technology, Julia Angwin has published the book Stealing MySpace about the rise and power of the social networking site MySpace and, as a columnist for the Wall Street Journal, she writes about technology. In this 2009 article from the *Wall Street Journal*, she writes about joining Twitter, finding followers, and distinguishing them from friends.

Readings for Writers: The Essay, "A Brother's Murder," by Brent Staples

In grieving for his murdered brother, the author remembers other black youths who never made it alive out of their economically deprived neighborhood. He mourns for the young men for whom gunplay has become a part of everyday life.

Readings for Writers: The Essay, "Navajo Code Talkers: The Century's Best- Kept Secret," by Jack Hitt

Since Navajo had never been written down or translated into an other language, it was a perfect choice for radio communication during World War II when the Japanese were able to break standard codes with ease. The Navajo Code Talkers translated military terms into words they knew from the reservation: a tank becoming a *turtle*, a hand grenade became a *potato*, and a fighter plane became a *hummingbird*. The United States won victories at several key points because of the secret communication these messages afforded our troops.

Additional Collaborative Exercise for Chapter Thirteen

1. Give groups of students an article and have them apply the reading process. You may choose from the essays in the textbook. Have them compare the items that they noticed during prereading and the items they marked during the rereading phase.

A Summary of the Reading Selections

Readings for Writers: "Manners Matter Online: Basic Etiquette Applies Even for E-Mail," by Amritha Alladi

Alladi wrote this article for the Gainesville (Florida) Sun, and she focuses on why students and other young people seeking employment need to sharpen their e-mail communication skills.

Readings for Writers: The Writing Process, "Getting Carded," by David Migoya

The essay explores a rite of passage for most Americans: getting their first credit card. The author warns that the card, a symbol of maturity, has its dangers.

Readings for Writers: Illustration, "A Life Full of Riches," by Karl R. Green

Karl R. Green lives in Cedar Rapids, Iowa. In this essay, originally published in Newsweek in 2007, Green gives many examples of the "riches" he enjoys. He notes, "This material world constantly reminds me of what I don't have. But somehow, I still feel wealthy."

Readings for Writers: Description, "The Colors," by Gary Soto

In this essay, Gary Soto describes his childhood world of Fresno, California. The Mexican-American poet, essayist, and short story writer relies heavily on the senses of sight, smell, sound, and touch as he writes of the summer days at his grandparents' house.

Readings for Writers: Narration, "The Good Father," by Alisa Valdes-Rodriguez

After overcoming a tumultuous childhood himself, the author's father becomes both mother and father to his own children. She thanks him with this essay which tells the story of her Cuban-born father.

Readings for Writers: Process, "Breath of Life," by Judith Sachs

After asserting that you can turn breathing into a meaningful twenty-minute activity that will help you get a deeper sense of yourself, Sachs describes the process of "creative breathing." In this essay, Sachs demonstrates how you can take a vacation from stress by performing the "Breath of Life" exercise, the process of which she describes in the essay.

Readings for Writers: Comparison or Contrast, "Honesty and Dishonesty" by Jo-Allen Dimitirus and Mark Mazzarella

This essay compares and contrasts the different kinds of liars, and it outlines the physical clues that occur when a person lies. The authors assert that honest people are relaxed and open in contrast to dishonest people, who are not.

Readings for Writers: Classification, "The Dog Ate My Disk, and Other Tales of Woe," by Carolyn Foster Segal

Carolyn Foster Segal originally wrote this article for *The Chronicle of Higher Education*, a magazine for college teachers. An English professor, Segal classifies student excuses according to the kind of misfortune they describe. Note that this essay was written for college teachers. See if you, as a student, find it amusing.

Readings for Writers: Definition, "Terrorism," by Ron Cunningham

Ron Cunningham is the editorial-page editor of the Gainesville (Florida) Sun. In this 2010 editorial, he defines terrorism in two ways: (1) as the national fear of flying, bombing, and other attacks by enemies abroad, and (2) as a fear that we ignore each time we drive. As he notes, "In a typical month, more of us are killed in traffic than perished in the attacks of 9–11." Consider whether his definitions make too little of global terrorism or make the reader think about highway safety.

Readings for Writers: Cause and Effect, "Say Something," by Lucie Prinz

Lucie Prinz writes about some adults' fear of teenagers and explains the effects of that fear. She uses two incidents, both of which take place on a subway, to ask why these adults are reluctant to interact with "the ordinary, harmless children we all come in contact with every day."

Readings for Writers: Argument, "The Case for a Tax on Sodas," by Jo Ivey Boufford

Boufford, president of the New York Academy of Medicine, writes about a growing concern in this country: the role of sugary drinks in the obesity epidemic. The statistics and studies in her article, published in 2010, are used to argue that a tax on sodas (combined with other programs and policies) could save lives.

Readings for Writers: The Essay, "How to Twitter," by Julia Angwin

Writing widely on issues of media and technology, Julia Angwin has published the book Stealing MySpace about the rise and power of the social networking site MySpace and, as a columnist for the Wall Street Journal, she writes about technology. In this 2009 article from the *Wall Street Journal*, she writes about joining Twitter, finding followers, and distinguishing them from friends.

Readings for Writers: The Essay, "A Brother's Murder" by Brent Staples

In grieving for his murdered brother, the author remembers other black youths who never made it alive out of their economically deprived neighborhood. He mourns for the young men for whom gunplay has become a part of everyday life.

Readings for Writers: The Essay, "Navajo Code Talkers: The Century's Best Kept Secret" by Jack Hitt

Since Navajo had never been written down or translated into another language, it was a perfect choice for radio communication during World War II when the Japanese were able to break standard codes with ease. The Navajo Code Talkers translated military terms into words they knew from the reservation, a tank becoming a *turtle*, a hand grenade becoming a *potato*, and a fighter plane becoming a *hummingbird*. The United States won victories at several key points because of the secret communication these messages afforded our troops.

Chapter One, Test A
Writing a Paragraph

Circle the correct answer.

1. Marking your first list of ideas and then clustering the related ideas into separate lists is
   _____.

   a) freewriting

   b) mapping

   c) brainstorming

   d) keeping a journal

2. The _____ summarizes the details in the paragraph.

   a) topic sentence

   b) topic

   c) outline

   d) map

3. The _____ is a plan to help you stay focused in your writing.

   a) map

   b) journal entry

   c) topic

   d) outline

4. What order is used when arguing a point?

   a) time order

   b) space order

   c) emphatic order

   d) step-by-step order

5. _____ means rewriting the draft of the paragraph to make changes in the structure and the
   order of sentences and content.

   a) Revising

   b) Editing

   c) Mapping

   d) Freewriting

6. _____ includes making changes in the choice of words, in the selection of details, in punctuation, and in the patterns and kinds of sentences.

a) Brainstorming

b) Freewriting

c) Editing

d) Revising

7. What are transitions?

a) journal entries

b) words, phrases, or sentences that link ideas

c) types of outlines

d) punctuation marks

8. When writing about an event, use _____ order.

a) time

b) emphatic

c) space

d) step-by-step

9. If you are describing a room, you might use _____ order.

a) time

b) emphatic

c) space

d) step-by-step order

10. _____ means that all the details relate to the topic sentence.

a) Support

b) Unity

c) Coherence

d) Brainstorming

11. _____ means all the details are listed in the right order.

a) Support

b) Unity

c) Transition

d) Coherence

12. When _____, give yourself fifteen minutes to write whatever comes to mind on your subject without stopping.

a) brainstorming

b) keeping a journal

c) mapping

d) freewriting

13. _____ means to pause to ask yourself questions that will lead to new ideas.

a) Freewriting

b) Brainstorming

c) Mapping

d) Outlining

14. _____ refers to editing and refining ideas.

a) Prewriting

b) Planning

c) Drafting

d) Polishing

15. _____ refers to generating and developing ideas for the paragraph.

a) Prewriting

b) Planning

c) Drafting

d) Polishing

I. Label the following topic sentences:

      OK – good topic sentence

      N – too narrow

      B – too broad

      A – announcement

1. _____ This essay is about the recent hurricane.

2. _____ My neighborhood changed a great deal.

3. _____ Jack likes oatmeal cookies.

4. _____ Philip is an avid sportsman.

5. _____ I live thirty minutes from my job.

6. _____ Our neighbor recycle cans and bottles.

7. _____ Vegetables are a source of vitamins.

8. _____ The Internet provides useful information.

9. _____ The subject of my paragraph will be gardening.

10. _____ The college's strict attendance policy causes problems for students.

II. Put an X beside details that do not support the topic sentence.

11. Topic Sentence: A birthday party requires careful planning.

    _____ Invitations must be mailed.

    _____ The host must prepare a menu and go shopping.

    _____ Some guests do not bring gifts.

    _____ Entertainment for the guests must be considered.

    _____ The hostess is not always shown appreciation for her hard work.

    _____ The guest list needs to be created.

    _____ Guests expect colorful decorations.

III. The following list contains topics and topic sentences. Label topics T; label topic sentences TS.

12. a._____ How to grow tomatoes.

    b._____ My wedding day.

    c._____ Valuable items can be discovered at garage sales.

    d._____ Three warning signs of alcoholism.

    e._____ Attending college provides several ways to meet people.

IV. Add three details to support the topic sentence.

Topic sentence: Numerous sounds can be heard in the mall during the Christmas holiday.

13._____

14._____

15._____

Chapter Two, Test A
Illustration

I. Circle the correct answer.

1. A _____ is a broad point.

a) specific example

b) general statement

c) topic sentence

d) transition

2. A(n) _____ paragraph uses specific examples to support a general point.

a) illustration

b) argument

c) process

d) description

3. Which of the following is a transition for an illustration paragraph?

a) equally

b) meanwhile

c) another instance

d) in contrast to

4. Which of the following is a transition for an illustration paragraph?

a) unlike

b) similarly

c) immediately

d) a second example

5. _____ are words, phrases, or sentences that connect one idea to another.

a) Specific statements

b) Transitions

c) General statements

d) Topics

6. Cable television offers a wide variety of programs.

    Which of the following examples does not support this general statement?

a) Several channels show music videos.

b) Children can watch cartoons on numerous channels.

c) Some channels show only sports such as football, tennis, or golf.

d) Cable has become expensive because of additional programming.

7. Our neighbors showed my family how much they cared when our home was destroyed by a fire.

    Which of the following examples does not support this general statement?

a) We have several generous neighbors.

b) Ms. Jones cooked meals for us each day.

c) The Williams family let us sleep in their guest bedroom.

d) Mr. Parker supplied lumber to rebuild our house.

8. Which of the following is not a transition for an illustration paragraph?

a) for example

b) like

c) in addition

d) immediately

9. Which of the following is not an important question you should consider when revising an illustration paragraph?

a) Should some of the sentences be combined?

b) Do I need better transitions?

c) Have I explained the steps clearly?

d) Should I add more details to support my point?

II. Add three appropriate details that support the following topic sentences.

10. Many people get nervous when they must speak to a large audience.

    1. _____

2. _____

3. _____

11. Planning a vacation can be stressful.

    1. _____

    2. _____

    3. _____

12. Listening to music is a great way to relax.

    1. _____

    2. _____

    3. _____

13. Good neighbors are an essential ingredient of a safe community.

    1. _____

    2. _____

    3. _____

14. College students are often stressed out during final-exam week.

    1. _____

2._____

3._____

15. Many people like going to amusement parks.

1._____

2._____

3._____

Chapter Two, Test B
Illustration

I. Create four specific examples for each broad statement.

Cellular phones have become a necessity in many people's lives.

1. _____

2. _____

3. _____

4. _____

The mall is more than just a place to shop.

5. _____

6. _____

7. _____

8. _____

The student body on college campuses has become quite diverse.

9. _____

10. _____

11. _____

12. _____

II. Create a topic sentence for each group of details.

13. _____

My daughter is involved in several sports with practice after school.

My husband works late almost every day.

The baby usually takes a nap just before dark.

I am exhausted after working all day, so I go to bed early.

The family eats together only during holidays and special occasions.

14. _____

Many colleges offer voice lessons.

Students can take beginner, intermediate, and advanced piano lessons.

Students receive college credit for performing in the marching band.

The most talented singers may audition for the college choir.

The pep band travels with the athletes and performs at games.

Musicians represent the college in parades and other special events.

III. Add three details to each topic sentence for an illustration paragraph.

The Internet can be a source of valuable information.

15. _____

16 _____

17. _____

The Internet can be a negative influence for some people.

18. _____

19. _____

20. _____

Chapter Three Test A
Description

I. Select the correct answer.

1. If a word or phrase is specific, it is _____ .

a) exact and precise

b) fuzzy

c) vague

d) general

2. Which of the following words is specific?

a) good

b) nice

c) courteous

d) bad

3. Which of the following is a general term?

a) rabbit

b) deer

c) cat

d) mammal

4. _____ shows a reader what a person, place, thing, or situation is like.

a) Process

b) Description

c) Classification

d) Cause and effect

5. The main point of the description is the _____ .

a) dominant impression

b) sense word

c) spatial position

d) time sequence

6. _____ means to organize descriptions from first to last.

a) Spatial position

b) Time sequence

c) Similar types

d) Dominant impression

7. Use _____ to organize descriptions from top to bottom or left to right.

a) spatial position

b) time sequence

c) similar types

d) argument

8. To describe related items, use _____.

a) spatial position

b) time sequence

c) similar types

d) narration

9. Which of the following is not used to devise sense detail?

a) colors

b) texture

c) odors

d) causes

10. Which of the following is not used to devise sense detail?

a) effects

b) roughness

c) noise

d) brightness

11. Which of the following is not a transition for a description paragraph?

a) in contrast

b) nearby

c) for this reason

d) beneath

12. Which of the following is not a transition for a description paragraph?

a) consequently

b) also

c) similarly

d) next to

13. When utilizing description, your writing should_____ and not tell.

a) explain

b) illustrate

c) analyze

d) show

14. Which of the following is a precise term?

a) cup

b) laptop computer

c) book

d) desk

15. Which of the following is a general term?

a) Christmas Tree

b) high school dance

c) home

d) ballet recital

Chapter Three Test B
Description

I. Place an X beside the general term in each list of words.

1. ____ baseball cards   2. ____ kitchen

     ____ collector's items   ____ nursery

     ____ stamps   ____ rooms

     ____ coins   ____ bedroom

     ____ dolls   ____ den

II. List three specific words for each general term.

3. general word: flower   4. general word: athlete

     _____   _____

     _____   _____

     _____   _____

III. Create a dominant impression from the list of details.

5. Dominant impression: _____

a. Baby toys were scattered on the living room floor.

b. The distinctive smell of a diaper pail filled the air.

c. Used bottles cluttered the sink.

d. A large playpen was erected in the center of the room.

IV. Place an X beside details that do not fit the dominant impression.

6. Dominant impression: The daycare center was the model of inefficiency.

     ____ Unsupervised children ran from one room to another.

     ____ The lock on the gate was broken.

     ____ Two infants slept in their cribs.

     ____ Only one smoke detector was in working order.

     ____ Medical records were not updated.

     ____ A baby was crying.

V. Create three details for the dominant impression.

Dominant impression: The student giving the speech was quite nervous.

7. _____

8. _____

9. _____

VI. Which type of order is used in the example? _____

10. It started to rain before we got out of bed. When the storm ended, all of our equipment was soaked. After realizing that the trip was ruined, we decided to go home.

Chapter Four, Test A

Narration

I. Circle the correct answer.

1. _____means telling a story.

a) Description

b) Illustration

c) Narration

d) Comparison

2. To get to the point of a narrative, which of the following is not a question to ask?

a) What did I learn?

b) What emotion did it make me feel?

c) Did it change me?

d) What is the next step?

3. Which of the following is not a rule for narration?

a) Pick a big topic.

b) Be interesting.

c) Stay in order.

d) Be clear.

4. Put _____ around a person's exact words.

a) commas

b) quotation marks

c) parentheses

d) dashes

5. Which of the following is not a transition for a narrative paragraph?

a) during

b) soon after

c) before

d) similarly

6. Which of the following is not a transition for a narrative paragraph?

a) on the other hand

b) at once

c) next

d) suddenly

7. How is a narrative different from a description?

a) A narrative relies on separate details.

b) A narrative is a type of paragraph.

c) A narrative covers an event in a time sequence.

d) A narrative contains transitions.

8. The point of the narrative is included in the _____.

a) details

b) topic sentence

c) title

d) action

9. Which of the following cannot be the topic sentence of a narrative paragraph?

a) I learned the importance of good study habits after I failed my final exam.

b) My wedding day was the happiest day of my life.

c) My first year as a parent taught me patience.

d) My court appearance changed my belief that all lawyers are dishonest.

10. What order is used in narration to organize detail?

a) time order

b) spatial order

c) most important to least important

d) least important to most important

11. Which of the following is an appropriate topic sentence of a narrative paragraph?

a) Winning is everything.

b) I want to tell you about my dog.

c) My mother is forty years old.

d) Getting robbed at gunpoint at the tender age of thirteen made me suspicious of all strangers.

12. Which of the following is a rule for narration?

a) Be clear.

b) Do not use quotations

c) Pick a boring topic.

d) Compare and contrast ideas.

13. Which of the following sentences utilizes a person's exact words appropriately?

a) Donna told me that "she didn't feel well."

b) "You're getting on my last nerve," said Julio.

c) Please tell Chris "to fix the car.

d) She said to budget the money appropriately."

14. Which of the following is not an appropriate way to gather details for a narrative paragraph?

a) freewriting

b) brainstorming

c) grouping ideas

d) memorizing

15. Which of the following is an appropriate topic sentence of a narrative paragraph?

a) My sister is in college.

b) I liked living in Florida.

c) Two dogs are in my driveway.

d) Making lunches for the homeless made me appreciate my house and the comforts it provides.

Narration

I. Some of the following sentences are good topic sentences for a narrative. Some are too big to develop in one paragraph, or they are too narrow to be developed. Some make no point. Place an X beside good topic sentences.

1. a.___ I learned to be responsible during the six years I spent in New York.

   b.___ My mother demonstrated true strength when our house was destroyed in a fire.

   c.___ The care that I received at the hospital after my accident eliminated my mistrust of doctors.

   d.___ Bob decided to work during summer vacation.

   e.___ Two men were charged with the crime.

   f.___ Graduating from high school was the happiest moment of my life.

   g.___ My pregnancy was a nightmare.

   h.___ Mike was extremely frightened during his first roller coaster ride.

   i.___ Three weeks at summer camp taught me the value of friendship.

   j.___ My first day at my new job taught me the importance of teamwork.

II. Punctuate the speaker's exact words.

2.   Logan said Be careful when you cross the street.

3.   Don't talk with food in your mouth Mom told us.

III. Create a topic sentence for the list of details.

4. Topic sentence: _____

_____

The bully walked through the park looking for a victim.

He spotted little Marco on the swings.

The bully called Marco a baby and pushed him off the swing.

Marco didn't cry or run away.

He told the bully that he would not fight him.

Marco suggested that they share the swing or play a game together.

The bully just smiled and walked away.

IV. Cross out the irrelevant details in the narrative outline.

5. Topic sentence: I learned the hard way that looks can be deceiving.

I spent several hours getting ready for my best friend's party.

I wanted my hair and clothes to be perfect because I knew my boyfriend Bobby would be there.

Cathy served pizza and soda at the party.

When I arrived, I saw him sitting in the corner with a girl I didn't know.

Bobby leaned over and whispered something in the girl's ear.

They both laughed.

Several kids were dancing close to me.

I immediately became angry and began to yell at him.

When I finally stopped screaming, the girl was crying, and everyone was watching us.

She was wearing a red- and- white dress.

She told me that Bobby was her cousin and had been trying to make her feel comfortable because she didn't know anyone at the party.

Afterwards, neither Bobby nor Cathy would speak to me.

I will never again jump to conclusions until I have all of the facts.

Chapter Five, Test A
Process

I. Select the correct answer.

1. A(n) _____ paragraph explains how to do something or describes how something happens or is done.

a) description

b) narration

c) process

d) illustration

2. A(n) _____ tells the reader how to do something.

a) directional process

b) topic

c) informational process

d) illustration paragraph

3. What explains how something happens or is done?

a) a directional process

b) an informational process

c) the grammatical person

d) illustration

4. Which of the following is not a hint for writing a process paragraph?

a) Include all the steps.

b) Find an activity you know well.

c) Put the steps in the right order.

d) Choose a topic that includes steps that do not have to be done in a specific time sequence.

5. Sentences in a directional process use the pronoun _____.

a) he

b) she

c) you

d) I

6. Which pronoun is not used in an informational process?

a) we

b) you

c) they

d) it

7. Mixing the two processes is called a _____.

a) process shift

b) singular shift

c) plural shift

d) shift in person

8. Which of the following is not a transition for a process paragraph?

a) similarly

b) first

c) sometimes

d) while I am

9. Which of the following is not a transition for a process paragraph?

a) as soon as

b) another case

c) begin by

d) at last

10. Which of the following is a first- person-singular pronoun?

a) you

b) they

c) I

d) we

11. Which of the following is a second- person- plural pronoun?

a) he

b) we

c) I

d) you

12. Which of the following is a third- person- singular pronoun?

a) it

b) they

c) you

d) we

13. Which of the following is a first- person- plural pronoun?

a) I

b) we

c) you

d) they

14. Which of the following is a second- person- singular pronoun?

a) it

b) she

c) you

d) they

15. Which of the following is a second- person- plural pronoun?

a) he

b) you

c) we

d) I

Chapter Five, Test B
Process

I. Name the types of processes that are illustrated in the following examples.

1. _____ Magma, melted rock inside the earth, rises to the surface. It moves up through a channel called a conduit. When the magma reaches the surface, gas is released.

2. _____ At the second traffic light, turn left. Follow this road for two miles. Look for a green house on your right.

II. Label the following topic sentences for a process paragraph.

  OK – good topic sentence

  A – announcement

  B – too broad

  S – topic does not require steps that must follow a specific order

3. _____ Programming a VCR is easy if you follow five steps.

4. _____ Numerous steps are involved in building a computer.

5. _____ This paragraph explains how to grow roses.

6. _____ There are several ways to meet people.

7. _____ By following a few simple steps, you can save money by changing the oil in your car.

8. _____ I will discuss the steps in making lasagna.

9. _____ Certain steps must be followed to build a house.

10. _____ Mary has a set routine for cleaning her closets.

11. _____ The formation of a hurricane follows a specific order.

12. _____ Tracey learned how to prepare several dishes.

III. Put the steps in the outline in the proper order.

Topic sentence: Bill follows a specific routine when he cuts his hair.

13._____ He always trims the hair over his ears first.

14._____ The supplies are put away.

15._____ After the long hair is cut, he trims the short hair.

16._____ Before cutting begins, he arranges all of his supplies on the counter.

17._____ He goes outside to show off his handiwork.

18._____ Hair clippings are cleaned from the razors.

19._____ He then cuts the long hair on top of his head.

IV. Correct shifts in person.

Styling my daughter's hair can be a challenge. Daria hates to have her hair combed, so I have to chase her through the house and catch her in order to begin. I hold her tightly to keep her on the chair. If you loosen your grip, she will bolt for the door. First, you comb out all of the tangles. This always makes her squirm and scream; however, you can't stop. Part her hair in the middle. I make two braids and secure them at the ends with colorful barrettes. Daria does not bother to thank you. She just glares at you and then runs outside to play.

Chapter Six, Test A
Comparison or Contrast

1. To _____ means to point out similarities.

a) narrate

b) compare

c) illustrate

d) contrast

2. To _____ means to point out differences.

a) argue

b) compare

c) contrast

d) narrate

3. Which pattern for organizing comparison or contrast paragraphs explains the topic sentence by first discussing all the details on one subject and then all the details on the other subject?

a) subject-by-subject

b) point-by-point

c) definition

d) spatial

4. Which pattern for organizing comparison or contrast paragraphs discusses each point, switching back and forth between subjects?

a) emphatic

b) spatial

c) subject-by-subject

d) point-by-point

5. In comparison or contrast paragraphs, _____.

a) use different points to compare and contrast subjects

b) give roughly equal space to both subjects

c) mix point-by-point and subject-by-subject patterns

d) use an obvious topic

6. In comparison or contrast paragraphs, _____.

a) make your point in the topic sentence

b) do not limit your topic

c) avoid transitions

d) use different points to compare subjects

7. Which of the following is not a transition for a comparison paragraph?

a) additionally

b) likewise

c) however

d) similar to

8. Which of the following is not a transition for a comparison paragraph?

a) in addition

b) as well as

c) equally

d) on the other hand

9. Which of the following is not a transition for a contrast paragraph?

a) although

b) like

c) otherwise

d) in contrast to

10. Which of the following is not a transition for a contrast paragraph?

a) both

b) conversely

c) except

d) whereas

11. Be sure to _____ when comparing or contrasting.

a) use unequal space for both subjects

b) use different points for both subjects

c) cover both topics in the topic sentence

d) make your point in the concluding sentence

12. Which sentence makes a suitable topic for a comparison or contrast paragraph?

a) My mother enjoys bicycling in the winter.

b) On the one hand, I hate broccoli, and on the other hand, I will eat broccoli if my mother makes me.

c) There are three dogs in my neighborhood.

d) My father was a stricter disciplinarian than my mother.

13. Which of the following is not included in the checklist for revising a comparison or contrast paragraph?

a. Did I include a topic sentence that covers both subjects?

b. Did I make a valid argument?

c. Do all details fit?

d. Are both subjects given roughly the same amount of space?

14. Which of the following transitions is not used to show differences?

a) equally

b) conversely

c) otherwise

d) still

15. Which of the following transitions is not used to show similarities?

a. also

b. like

c. nevertheless

d. too

Chapter Six, Test B
Comparison or Contrast

I. Define the following terms.

1. **compare** _____

2. **contrast** _____

II. For the pairs of sentences, decide whether they show comparison or contrast. Then combine the two using an appropriate transition.

3. We had to buy expensive camera equipment for the photography class.

   We needed only a calculator for the accounting class.

   _____

   _____

4. Rick spends his entire vacation at the beach.

   Mike goes to the beach on weekends and each day after work.

   _____

   _____

5. Young girls swooned when they listened to songs by Elvis Presley in the 50s.

   Teenage girls fainted when Michael Jackson performed in the 90s.

   _____

   _____

6. The entertainment section of the newspaper gives a brief summary of current movies.

   Movie critics on television discuss the actors, the plot, and the director in detail.

   _____

   _____

III. Create a topic sentence from the list of details.

7. Topic sentence_____

	Army Basic Training	**Marine Corps Boot Camp**
Training:	Soldiers learn survival skills and how to use weapons	Marines practice survival skills and how to use various weapons
Length:	Nine weeks	Ten weeks
Instructors:	Non-commissioned officers	Non-commissioned officers

8. Topic sentence_____

	Alligators	**Crocodiles**
Snout:	round	pointed
Teeth:	the fourth tooth fits into a pocket in the upper jaw	the fourth tooth fits into a groove outside the mouth
Head:	short and flat	long and narrow

IV. Name the patterns used to organize comparison or contrast essays.

9. _____

10. _____

Chapter Seven Test A
Classification

1. Classify mean to divide something into different categories according to _____.

a) a dominant impression

b) spatial order

c) emphatic order

d) a basis

2. When writing a classification paragraph, divide the subject into _____ categories.

a) three or more

b) two

c) one

d) one or two

3. Which of the following is not a hint for writing a classification paragraph?

a) pick one basis for classification

b) be creative in your classification

c) pick two or more bases for classification

d) have a reason for your classification

4. Which of the following is not used when creating a topic sentence for a classification paragraph?

a) a question about the basis for classification

b) what is being classified

c) the basis for classification

d) the categories

5. To classify shoes using the different occasions that they are worn as the basis for classification, which of the following categories does not fit?

a) athletic shoes

b) shoes for formal wear

c) leather shoes

d) work shoes

6. To classify chores using the level of difficulty as the basis for classification, which of the following categories does not fit?

a) very difficult chores

b) outdoor chores

c) moderately difficult chores

d) easy chores

7. To classify purses using the material from which they are made as the basis for classification, which of the following categories does not fit?

a) designer purses

b) leather purses

c) canvas purses

d) plastic purses

8. Which word cannot be used in a classification paragraph as an alternate word for *kind* or *type*?

a) class

b) group

c) species

d) draft

9. To classify cars using the maker as the basis for classification, which of the following categories does not fit?

a) Ford

b) General Motors

c) convertible

d) Chrysler

10. The topic sentence for a classification paragraph should mention:

a) what is being classified.

b) specific details and steps

c) information about the type of classification

d) point-by-point comparisons

11. To classify movies using the type as the basis for classification, which of the following categories does not fit?

a) action

b) "The Terminator"

c) drama

d) supernatural thriller

12. To classify on-air TV shows using the time of day a show airs as basis for classification, which of the following categories does not fit?

a) morning shows

b) late night talk shows

c) reality shows

d) mid-day news

13. To classify academic degrees using the type of degree as the basis for classification, which of the following categories does not fit?

a) bachelor's

b) master's

c) associate's

d) liberal arts

14. To classify nail polish using color as the basis for classification, which of the following categories does not fit?

a) Maybelline

b) red

c) brown

d) purple

15. To classify teachers using where they teach as the basis for classification, which of the following categories does not fit?

a) English teacher

b) high-school teacher

c) college professor

d) middle-school teacher

Chapter Seven Test B

Classification

I. Give the basis for classification for each list below.

1. topic: furniture

    basis for classification _____

    categories: bedroom

    nursery

    dining room

    den

2. topic: scary movies

    basis for classification_____

    categories: mummy

    werewolf

    ghost

    demon

3. topic: hotels

    basis for classification _____

    categories: expensive

    moderately expensive

    inexpensive

II. Give three categories that fit the basis for classification.

topic: toys

basis for classification: age groups of people who use them

4._____

5._____

6._____

topic: salespeople

basis for classification: type of service provided

7._____

8._____

9._____

topic: dancers

basis for classification: types of dances they do

10._____

11._____

12._____

III. Write a topic sentence that mentions the basis for classification.

13. _____

Write a topic sentence that mentions the categories.

14._____

Write a topic sentence that includes the basis for classification and the categories.

15._____

Chapter Eight Test A
Definition

A _____ paragraph is one that explains what a term means to you.

a) description

b) definition

c) narrative

d) process

2. Which of the following is not a way to explain the meaning of a term?

a) give examples

b) tell a story

c) contrast your term with another

d) use only the dictionary

3. Which of the following is not a part of the topic sentence for a definition paragraph?

a) the dominant impression

b) the term

c) the broad class or category

d) distinguishing characteristics

4. _____ terms refer to things you can see, touch, taste, smell, or hear.

a) Abstract

b) Absolute

c) Concrete

d) Connection

5. _____ terms refer to things that cannot be seen, touched, tasted, smelled, or heard.

a) Abstract

b) Absolute

c) Concrete

d) Connection

6. Which of the following should not be chosen as a term to define?

a) a personal quality you admire

b) a personal quality you dislike

c) a quality that provokes a strong reaction in you

d) a term that can be quickly defined

7. Avoid defining one abstract term by using _____.

a) a story

b) another abstract term

c) examples

d) contrast with another term

8. In the topic sentence of a definition paragraph, the broad class or category should _____.

a) follow the distinguishing characteristics

b) follow the personal attitude

c) follow the term

d) come before the term

9. In the topic sentence of a definition paragraph, the term should _____.

a) be first

b) follow the broad class

c) follow the category

d) follow the distinguishing characteristics

10. Which of the following is not a good choice of a term to define?

a) fear

b) cabbage

c) a workaholic

d) boredom

Chapter Eight Test B
Definition

I. What three items must be in the topic sentence of a definition paragraph?

1. _____

2. _____

3. _____

II. Complete the topic sentences for a definition paragraph.

4. A bully is a _____ who _____

_____

5. A snob is a _____ who _____

_____

6. A tattletale is a _____ who _____

_____

III. Rewrite the abstract sentences and give them concrete language.

7. Jake is always there for me when I need him.

8. Brenda sacrifices her time for those in need.

9. My uncle is truly generous.

IV. In the list below, place an A beside abstract words and a C beside concrete words.

10. ____ optimism	14. ____ stereo	18. ____ television
11. ____ volcano	15. ____ vegetable	19. ____ patriotism
12. ____ pride	16. ____ failure	20. ____ dictionary
13. ____ grief	17. ____ comfort	

Chapter Nine Test A
Cause and Effect

1. When you are writing about the reasons for something, you are writing _____.

a) definition

b) effect

c) cause

d) narration

2. When you are writing about the results of something, you are writing _____.

a) effect

b) cause

c) illustration

d) description

3. Which of the following topics is appropriate for a cause paragraph?

a) why people commit crimes

b) why I attend college

c) causes of unemployment growth

d) causes of disease

4. Which of the following topics is appropriate for an effect paragraph?

a) effects of immunization

b) effects of recycling

c) effects of violence on children

d) effects of recycling in my neighborhood

5. Try to have at least _____ causes or effects in your paragraph.

a) three

b) five

c) six

d) two

6. Which of the following is not a word that signals causes?

a) reasons

b) why

c) impact

d) motives

7. Which of the following is not a word that signals causes?

a) because

b) changed

c) intentions

d) reasons

8. Which of the following is not a word that signals effects?

a) results

b) intentions

c) consequences

d) improved

9. Which of the following is not a word that signals effects?

a) threatened

b) changed

c) impact

d) why

10. If you are writing about some immediate and some long-range effects, you should discuss the effects in _____ .

a) time order

b) emphatic order

c) logical order

d) step-by-step order

11. If one cause leads to another, use _____.

a) time order

b) emphatic order

c) logical order

d) step-by-step order

12. Saving the most important effect for last is using _____.

a) time order

b) emphatic order

c) logical order

d) mixed order

13. Which of the following is not a transition for a cause paragraph?

a) because

b) due to

c) for this reason

d) consequently

14. Which of the following is not a transition for an effect paragraph?

a) since

b) as a result

c) therefore

d) in consequence

15. You should have at least _____ causes or effects in a cause or effect paragraph.

a) one

b) two

c) three

d) four

Chapter Nine Test B
Cause and Effect

I. Place a C next to topic sentences for cause paragraphs. Place an E next to topic sentences for effect paragraphs.

1. ____ I was overwhelmed by the consequences of working part time while attending college.
2. ____ Bertha's father established a curfew because she stayed out too late, neglected her studies, and ignored her chores.
3. ____ The mayor had several motives for canceling the fund-raiser.
4. ____ Teens experiment with drugs because of peer pressure, low self-esteem, and curiosity.
5. ____ I was not prepared for the results of buying a used car.
6. ____ Moving to a large city changed my social behavior.
7. ____ The taste, smell, and appearance of the food caused me to lose my appetite.
8. ____ The renovations improved the appearance of the museum.
9. ____ The installation of our backyard pool attracted neighborhood kids, depleted our savings, and raised our property value.
10. ____ Martha and Ted have several reasons for adopting a child.

II. For each of the topic sentences, create four causes or four effects depending upon what is required.

Topic sentence: Having kids has changed my morning routine.

11. _____
12. _____
13. _____
14. _____

Topic sentence: Students do poorly in school for many reasons.

15. _____
16. _____
17. _____
18. _____

III. Write a topic sentence for each outline.

19. Topic sentence _____

   _____

      Jessica never agreed with her boss.

      He criticized all of her suggestions.

      She lived in another town.

      She had to get up early for the long commute to work.

      Jessica received a job offer from another company.

      The salary at the new job was higher than her current salary.

20. Topic sentence _____

   _____

      Eating too much candy caused my teeth to decay.

      Six of my teeth have fallen out.

      Potato chips and soda do not give me enough energy to leave the house or exercise.

      I have been overweight since I was a child.

      Eating too much fried food has raised my cholesterol above recommended levels.

      My doctor informed me that my blood pressure has continued to rise.

Chapter Ten Test A
Argument

1. A(n) _____ is an attempt to persuade a reader to think or act in a certain way.

a) argument

b) description

c) narrative

d) process

2. What must be in the topic sentence of an argument paragraph?

a) only the subject

b) only the stand being taken

c) the subject and the stand being taken

d) the subject and opponents' stand

3. Which of the following is not a hint for writing a topic sentence?

a) Consider the audience.

b) Pick a topic based on someone else's experiences.

c) Pick a topic you can handle.

d) Consider your audience.

4. To _____ means to prove that an objection isn't valid.

a) concede

b) validate

c) repose

d) refute

5. To _____ a point means to admit that the other side has a point.

a) refute

b) concede

c) acknowledge

d) collate

6. Which of the following does not apply to reasons in argument?

a) clear

b) specific

c) vague

d) logical

7. Try to come up with at least _____ reason(s) for your position.

a) three

b) two

c) one

d) six

8. Saving the best reason for last is using _____.

a) spatial order

b) chronological order

c) step-by-step order

d) emphatic order

9. Which of the following is not a transition to use for emphasis?

a) finally

b) mainly

c) next

d) primarily

10. Which of the following is not a transition to use for emphasis?

a) in the meantime

b) most significant

c) most important

d) above all

11. When writing a persuasive paragraph, you should consider your _____.
a) description
b) narration
c) audience
d) announcement

12. Which of the following is a good topic sentence for an argument paragraph?
a) There are several types of tropical fruit that can be grown in cold weather.
b) I learned diligence, patience, and reverence while working at the monestary.
c) Several months ago, I got my first part-time job.
d) Teenagers should not attend college during the year they graduate from high school because many teens would benefit from a year of travel and exploration.

13. Select the best support for the following topic sentence: Household pets should not be allowed on airplanes.
a) Some passengers don't like cats.
b) Pets could get out of their carrying cases, run up and down the aisles, and pose added safety concerns for the plane's crew and passengers; thereby, they could increase the risk of a plane crash.
c) Barking dogs are irritating.
d) Pets might get motion sickness.

14. Which of the following is not a transition for a persuasive paragraph?
a) in comparison
b) most important
c) however
d) primarily

15. Select the best support for the following topic sentence: Parents should not spank children because childhood spankings result in angry, violent, dysfunctional adults.
a) Some dysfunctional adults were not spanked as children.
b) Sometimes spanking doesn't hurt kids.
c) Research indicates that children who received spankings were twice as likely once they became adults to be convicted of a violent crime.
d) My next door neighbor was spanked as a child, yet he is the kindness person on my block.

Chapter Ten Test B
Argument

I. Label the following topic sentences for argument paragraphs.

OK – good topic sentence

L – too large or research required

A – announcement

S – does not take a stand

1. ____ Senior citizens are often the victims of scams.

2. ____ Jefferson High School should require a school uniform.

3. ____ U.S. subsidies to Third World countries need more regulation.

4. ____ The reasons to eliminate fund-raisers at the school will be discussed in this paragraph.

5. ____ Political wrongdoing in foreign countries should be investigated.

6. ____ Patricia Murphy should be elected as city councilwoman.

7. ____ Drinking and driving is a serious problem.

8. ____ The subject of this paper is extending the mall's hours of operation.

9. ____ The tenement is overrun with rats and roaches.

10.____ Vending machines selling junk food should be removed from elementary schools.

II. Place an X beside the most significant reason in each list.

11. Jacksonville should build a youth recreation center.

    a. _____ The center will allow kids to meet new people.

    b. _____ By keeping them off the streets, the center will provide a safe environment where kids can play.

    c. _____ Kids can play sports instead of just watching television after school.

12. Our landlord should not conduct monthly inspections of the rental property.

    a. _____ Tenants who have jobs must adjust their work schedules if they want to be at home during inspections.

    b. _____ Most property owners conduct only quarterly inspections.

    c. _____ The landlord will lose money if tenants move out because of the constant intrusions.

III. Place an X beside reasons that overlap.

13. Topic sentence: Teachers in public schools deserve salary increases.

    a. ____ Teachers are required to perform school-related activities after work.

    b. ____ Teachers provide a valuable service, yet they are grouped with the lowest-paid professionals in the country.

    c. ____ Many teachers grade papers and prepare for the next day's classes at home.

    d. ____ A salary increase would help to reduce teacher shortages in schools.

14. Topic sentence: The parking lot next to the auditorium needs to be paved.

    a. ____ People do not attend functions there because they fear damage to their cars.

    b. ____ After rainstorms, most of the lot is covered in mud.

    c. ____ People who park in other areas risk injury when they cross the busy street in front of the auditorium.

    d. ____ Tires are often punctured by objects hidden in the grass.

IV. Place an X beside the reason that is not specific.

15. State officials need to increase the punishment for D.U.I. offenses.

    a. ____ Accidents and deaths caused by drunk drivers will decrease.

    b. ____ Drivers will be more likely to appoint designated drivers.

    c. ____ Clubs and bars would be affected.

16. Parents should monitor what their children watch on television.

    a. ____ Some commercials can be bad.

    b. ____ Many shows contain extreme acts of violence that children may re-enact.

    c. ____ Television shows present morals that are not acceptable in some homes.

V. Give two reasons to support each point.

Topic sentence: School officials should begin random searches of school lockers.

17. _____

18. _____

Topic sentence: The cafeteria should install vending machines.

19. _____

20. _____

Chapter Eleven Test A
Writing an Essay

1. The main point of the essay is the _____.

a) subpoint

b) paragraph

c) body

d) thesis

2. The subpoints in an essay are the _____.

a) topic sentences

b) paragraphs

c) main points

d) topics

3. The first paragraph of the essay is usually the _____.

a) conclusion

b) introduction

c) body

d) topic sentence

4. Where does the thesis go in the essay?

a) conclusion

b) body

c) introduction

d) title

5. Which of the following is not a characteristic of the thesis?

a) The thesis does not announce.

b) The thesis is not too broad.

c) The thesis is not expressed in a sentence.

d) The thesis is not too narrow.

6. Which of the following is not true of the thesis statement?

a) You can mention the specific subpoints in the thesis.

b) You cannot make a point without listing the subpoints in the thesis.

c) You can make a point without listing the subpoints in the thesis.

d) The thesis should not be too narrow.

7. Which of the following is not a hint for outlining?

a) Focus on several points.

b) Check the topic sentence.

c) Include enough details.

d) Stay on one point.

8. Each topic sentence in each body paragraph should support the _____.

a) previous topic sentence

b) introduction

c) conclusion

d) thesis statement

9. _____ means that the paragraphs and details in each paragraph are in the most effective order.

a) Unity

b) Coherence

c) Support

d) Development

10. _____ means that the thesis and topic sentence all lead to the same point.

a) Support

b) Coherence

c) Unity

d) Development

11. Which of the following is not a hint for writing the introduction?

a) Never tell a story.

b) You can begin with general statements.

c) You can use one or more questions to lead into the thesis.

d) You can open with a contradiction of the main point.

12. Try to make your body paragraphs at least _____ sentences long.

a) ten

b) twelve

c) fifteen

d) seven

13. The last paragraph in the essay is the _____.

a) conclusion

b) introduction

c) body

d) thesis

14. Which of the following is not a strategy for writing the conclusion paragraph?

a) Restate the thesis in new words.

b) Rewrite the thesis as it appears in the introduction.

c) Make a judgment, valuation, or recommendation.

d) Frame the essay.

15. Which of the following is not a method used to link paragraphs?

a) restate an idea

b) use synonyms

c) avoid transitions

d) use repetition

Chapter Eleven Test B
Writing an Essay

I. Label the following topic sentences for an essay.

> OK – good topic sentence
>
> B – too broad
>
> N – too narrow
>
> A – announcement

1. _____ A steak dinner at 4:30 p.m. on Tuesday is good to eat.

2. _____ Refinishing a table can be accomplished in four steps.

3. _____ "Guns should be banned" is the topic of this essay.

4. _____ The colonization of Africa spanned several decades.

5. _____ A good nurse is patient, hardworking, and compassionate.

6. _____ This is about loyalty.

7. _____ Americans are addicted to many medications.

8. _____ Museums offer both entertainment and education.

9. _____ Caffeine in the winter months acts as a stimulant.

10. ___ Sororities and fraternities perform valuable services in the community.

II. Write a thesis statement for the list of subpoints.

11. _____

_____

    a. Microwave dishes can be prepared in a few minutes.

    b. There is a wide variety of meals.

    c. Microwave meals are inexpensive.

12. _____

_____

    a. The tuition at universities is higher than the tuition at community colleges.

    b. Community colleges generally have smaller classes than universities.

    c. Universities offer more specialized degrees than community colleges.

III. Write three topic sentences for each thesis statement.

13. Thesis statement: Misusing credit cards can cause numerous problems.

_____

_____

_____

14. Thesis statement: Maria did not display the qualities of a good salesperson.

_____

_____

_____

IV. Restate the thesis statement.

Thesis statement: Before selecting a college, a person should review the catalog, speak with college counselors, and tour the campus.

15. _____

_____

Chapter Twelve Test A
Different Essay Patterns: Part I

1. For illustration essays, use _____ to support a general statement.
a) specific examples
b) general statements
c) topics
d) broad examples

2. Divide the narrative essay into _____.
a) a body paragraph for every event that happens
b) several points
c) clear stages
d) body paragraphs only

3. There are _____ kinds of process essays.
a) four
b) two
c) three
d) five

4. When writing a description essay, _____.
a) develop a dominant impression
b) use few specific details
c) order of details is not important
d) transitions are not needed

5. Which of the following is not a hint for writing a comparison or contrast essay?
a) use the thesis to make a statement about the items being compared or contrasted
b) use the subject-by-subject method of organization
c) use the point-by-point method of organization
d) use the points of comparison or contrast to organize body paragraphs

6. When a writer is using the point-by-point pattern to organize a comparison or contrast essay, each _____ can explain one point of comparison or contrast.

a) sentence

b) body paragraph

c) conclusion

d) introduction

7. When a student is writing a descriptive essay, it is important to_____.

a) decide on a clear order

b) use many specific details

c) relate to the five senses of sight, sound, taste, touch (or texture), and smell.

d) all of the above

8. A directional process essay tells the reader_____

a) how to do something

b) an explanation of an activity

c) about an event

d) all of the above

9. One way to get started on a comparison or contrast essay is to _____.

a) list as many differences or similarities as you can on one topic

b) put events in chronological order

c) develop a list of transitions

d) all of the above

10. A narrative essay tells a _____.

a) point

b) story

c) thought

d) position

I. Write three topic sentences for each thesis statement.

My choice to work full time while attending college taught me to use my time wisely.

1. _____

2. _____

3. _____

Our town needs to build a new public library.

4. _____

5. _____

6. _____

II. Write a thesis statement for the topic sentences.

7. _____

    Rottweilers make great guard dogs.

    Contrary to popular belief, the dogs are good playmates for children.

    Rottweilers can be trained to perform numerous services.

8. _____

Drunk drivers are responsible for one/third of all highway accidents.

Many people convicted of driving under the influence are repeat offenders.

Hundreds of lives are lost each month because of drinking and driving.

III. Restate each thesis.

College is the ideal place to try new things.

9. _____

Video games can teach children valuable lessons about life.

10. _____

Chapter 13
Different Essay Patterns: Part II

Select the correct answer.

1. A simple way to structure a classification essay is to _____ .

a) explain each type in one paragraph

b) explain only one type

c) remove the basis for classification

d) explain each type in a separate body paragraph

2. Which of the following is not included in the thesis of a definition essay?

a) the term being defined

b) related terms

c) the broad class or category

d) specific distinguishing characteristics

3. Which of the following is not a hint for writing a cause or effect essay?

a) choose causes or effects

b) use each cause as the focus of one body paragraph

c) use all causes or effects in one body paragraph

d) use causes and effects in one essay

4. When writing an argument essay, _____ .

a) do not take a stand in the thesis

b) disregard the audience's objections

c) pick a topic based on your own experience and observation

d) take a stand in the conclusion

5. Which of the following is not a way to handle objections in an argument essay?

a) refute the objection

b) concede an objection

c) turn the objection into an advantage

d) ignore the objection

6. When you admit an objection is valid but use it to reinforce your own point, you are _____.

a) refuting the objection

b) turning the objection into an advantage

c) conceding the point

d) arguing poorly

7. When you prove that an objection isn't valid, you are _____.

a) conceding the point

b) turning the objection into an advantage

c) refuting the point

d) losing the argument

8. When writing definition essays, define a term that can be explained _____.

a) by more than the words in the dictionary

b) by the words in the dictionary

c) by research

d) without using personal feelings

9. For classification essays, divide the item into ___ type(s).

a) two

b) one

c) one to two

d) three or more

10. When you _____ an objection (that is, you can prove that it isn't valid), you have removed a major obstacle.

a)   refute
b)   concede
c)   criticize
d)   argue

Chapter Fourteen Test

Using Research to Strengthen Essay

I. Circle the correct answer.

1. Which of the following is not a source for obtaining research in a college library?

a) the card catalog
b) periodical indexes
c) Internet search engines
d) speaker's bureau

2. When obtaining research from the Internet, students often forget to check sources for _____.

a) timestamp
b) validity
c) URLs
d) author's name

3. When you provide documentation within a research essay, you are using _____.

a. quotations
b. AP Formatting
c. internal citations
d. Chicago Formatting

4. At the end of a documented essay, the _____ page lists all the sources cited in a paper.

a) Footnotes
b) Works Cited
c) Bibliography
d) Paraphrase

5. _____ occurs when you use a sources words or ideas and fail to give proper credit to the author or source of the work.

a) Plagiarism
b) Misquoting
c) Attribution
d) Direct quotation

6. Which of the following is not a signal phrase?

a) Dr. Lee notes
b) Professor James pointed out

c) Governor Madison claims

d) The examiner likes

II. Paraphrase each of the short excerpts below and include the appropriate parenthetical documentation. Use a signal phrase in each of the excerpts you paraphrase.

7. "Through all human needs both intimacy and independence, women tend to focus on the first and men the second. It is as if their lifeblood ran in different directions." (from You Just Don't Understand: Women and Men in Conversation, by Deborah Tannen, page 26)

_____

_____

_____

8. "Most Americans eat great quantities of food frequently, based on convenience. In fact, the entire fast-food and TV dinner industries have flourished due to our fast-paced lifestyles that demand we eat "convenient" foods." (from The Maker's Diet, by Jordan S. Rubin, page 31)

_____

_____

_____

9. "The increase in storm intensity in recent years has been tracked by the insurance industry which has been hit hard by recent disasters. Until the mid-1980s, it was widely thought that windstorms or hurricanes with insured losses exceeding one billion (thousand million) US dollars were only possible, if at all, in the United States." (from Global Warming: The Complete Briefing by John Houghton, page 4)

_____

_____

_____

10. "Indeed your chances of really getting where you want to go in life often hinge on your reaction to some shattering setback. Will you give up or will you keep on trying? It's as simple as that. And what you decide, decides your future. (from You Can If You Think You Can, by Norman Vincent Peale, page 4)

_____

_____

_____

11. "Despite the obstacles, some Americans manage to become financially independent each year without the state lottery, casinos, a big inheritance, or a successful business or invention. How? The answer, quite simply, is planning." (from <u>Saving on a Shoestring: How to Cut Expenses Reduce Debt and Stash More Cash</u>, by Barbara O'Neill, page 11)

_____

_____

_____

III. Arrange the items from the basic sources below in correct MLA format.

12. **Book**
   City where published: Lake Mary
   Publisher: Siloam
   Author: Jordan S. Rubin
   Title: The Maker's Diet
   Year: 2004

_____

_____

13. **Magazine article (from a monthly publication)**
   Article: Go Ahead, Say You're Sorry
   Author: Aaron Lazare
   Magazine: Psychology Today
   Pages: 40–45
   Month: January/February
   Year: 1995

_____

_____

14. Newspaper article

Newspaper: The New York Times
Article: Mexico Arrests Ex-Chief of Antidrug Agency
Date: Saturday, November 22, 2008
Page: A6
Writen by: Elisabeth Malkin

15. Journal article
Journal: Journal of Advanced Nursing
Article: Use of complementary and alternative medicine among people living with diabetes: literature review
Volume: 58
Issue Number: 4
Year Published: 2007
Pages: 307—319
Authors: Chang, Hsiao-yun; Wallis, Marianne; Tiralongo, Evelin

---

Chapter Fifteen Test A
The Simple Sentence

Identify the subject and verb of each sentence.

1. The children decided to play in the sandbox during recess.

a) children, decided to play

b) sandbox, during

c) children, decided

d) children, to play

2. During the show, nobody noticed the time.

a) nobody, noticed

b) show, noticed

c) show, during

d) time, noticed

3. The voters should have exited the polls by now.

a) voters, have exited

b) voters, should have exited

c) polls, exited

d) voters, should have

4. Bonnie and Clyde were famous criminals.

a) Bonnie and Clyde, were

b) Bonnie/Clyde, criminals

c) criminals, were

d) Bonnie/Clyde, were

5. After the party at my house, we cleaned for hours.

a) we, cleaned

b) party, for hours

c) house, cleaned

d) party, at

6. There is a salesman on the front porch.

a) salesman, there

b) salesman, is

c) porch, there is

d) salesman, there is

7. Juanita is not taking Stewart to the prom.

a) Juanita, is not taking

b) Juanita, is not

c) Juanita, is taking

d) Stewart, to

8. Did your son graduate from college in May?

a) son, graduate

b) son, did graduate

c) your, did graduate

d) son, did

9. The dog was barking at a stranger.

a) dog, barking

b) dog, was

c) stranger, at

d) dog, was barking

10. Have you ever visited another country?

a) you, have visited

b) you, have ever visited

c) you, have

d) you, ever visited

11. There are many reasons to stay at home tonight.

a) home, are

b) reasons, are

c) there, are

d) many, are

12. Beneath a loose board on the porch are my extra keys.

a) porch, are

b) board, are

c) keys, are

d) keys, beneath

13. Willie lifted the phone and asked for an overseas operator.

a) Willie, lifted/asked

b) Willie, lifted

c) Willie, asked

d) phone, asked

14. With a smile on his face, Dad invited me to eat with him.

a) smile, on

b) Dad, invited/to eat

c) me, to eat

d) Dad, invited

15. I should have studied for the test.

a) I, have studied

b) I, should have studied

c) test, should have studied

d) I, should have

Chapter Fifteen Test B
The Simple Sentence

Underline the subject and verb in each sentence. Put S above the subject and V above the verb.

1. Here are two copies of the exam.

2. Next to the theater are a camera shop and a pet store.

3. Juanita is concerned about her friend's illness.

4. John and his sister will visit their grandparents during summer vacation.

5. The puppy quickly chewed and swallowed its food.

6. Didn't you attend classes last summer?

7. In the closet beside the box is your birthday present.

8. The mayor will not approve the board's budget proposal.

9. There are several reasons for the increase in prices.

10. I should have been considered for the job opening.

11. Biking is an excellent form of exercise.

12. This soup tastes spicy.

13. Beverly always makes two cakes for the banquet.

14. A large turnout of voters is not expected at the polls today.

15. Mike and Ted never wash their mother's car.

16. We haven't studied for our Spanish exam.

17. I can hear the sound of music in the distance.

18. Flowers are blooming in the meadow beside our house.

19. Behind the tall buildings are a statue and a bench.

20. Will you attend the party for the new faculty members?

Chapter Sixteen Test A
Beyond the Simple Sentence: Coordination

Select the answer that is punctuated correctly.

1. I was late for my appointment so I accidentally ran a red light.

   a) I was late for my appointment so, I accidentally ran a red light.

   b) I was late for my appointment; so I accidentally ran a red light.

   c) I was late for my appointment, so, I accidentally ran a red light.

   d) I was late for my appointment, so I accidentally ran a red light.

2. Money was not a concern therefore we purchased souvenirs for everyone.

   a) Money was not a concern; therefore, we purchased souvenirs for everyone.

   b) Money was not a concern, therefore, we purchased souvenirs for everyone.

   c) Money was not a concern; therefore we purchased souvenirs for everyone.

   d) Money was not a concern, therefore; we purchased souvenirs for everyone.

3. The executives decided to downsize the company several employees lost jobs.

   a) The executives decided to downsize the company, several employees lost jobs.

   b) The executives decided to downsize the company; several employees lost jobs.

   c) The executives decided to downsize the company several; employees lost jobs.

   d) The executives decided to downsize the company, several, employees lost jobs.

4. I passed all of my final exams now I can prepare for graduation.

   a) I passed all of my final exams; now, I can prepare for graduation.

   b) I passed all of my final exams, now I can prepare for graduation.

   c) I passed all of my final exams; now I can prepare for graduation.

   d) I passed all of my final exams, now, I can prepare for graduation.

5. The fans crowded into the packed arena but the show was delayed for two hours.

a) The fans crowded into the packed arena, but the show was delayed for two hours.

b) The fans crowded into the packed arena but, the show was delayed for two hours.

c) The fans crowded into the packed arena; but the show was delayed for two hours.

d) The fans crowded into the packed arena; but, the show was delayed for two hours.

6. The water was too cold for swimming we didn't have anything to do.

a) The water was too cold for swimming, we, didn't have anything to do.

b) The water was too cold for swimming, we didn't have anything to do.

c) The water was too cold for swimming; we, didn't have anything to do.

d) The water was too cold for swimming; we didn't have anything to do.

7. Many sports fans don't mind cold weather therefore the stands are filled in December.

a) Many sports fans don't mind cold weather, therefore, the stands are filled in December.

b) Many sports fans don't mind cold weather; therefore, the stands are filled in December.

c) Many sports fans don't mind cold weather, therefore; the stands are filled in December.

d) Many sports fans don't mind cold weather, therefore the stands are filled in December.

8. I have never lived away from home in fact I have never spent the night away from home.

a) I have never lived away from home, in fact I have never spent the night away from home.

b) I have never lived away from home; in fact, I have never spent the night away from home.

c) I have never lived away from home, in fact, I have never spent the night away from home.

d) I have never lived away from home, in fact; I have never spent the night away from home.

9. Something happened to the battery and the car wouldn't start.

a) Something happened to the battery; and the car wouldn't start.

b) Something happened to the battery and the car wouldn't start.

c) Something happened to the battery, and the car wouldn't start.

d) Something happened to the battery, and, the car wouldn't start.

10. The little girl was very sick she was taken to the emergency room at the hospital.

a) The little girl was very sick she was taken to the emergency room at the hospital.

b) The little girl was very sick; she, was taken to the emergency room at the hospital.

c) The little girl was very sick she was taken; to the emergency room at the hospital.

d) The little girl was very sick; she was taken to the emergency room at the hospital.

11. I downloaded several files from the Internet for I had a report due on Monday.

a) I downloaded several files from the Internet, for I had a report due on Monday.

b) I downloaded several files from the Internet for, I had a report due on Monday.

c) I downloaded several files from the Internet; for I had a report due on Monday.

d) I downloaded several files from the Internet for I had a report due on Monday.

12. I studied two hours for the test as a result I was pleased with my grade.

a) I studied two hours for the test; as a result I was pleased with my grade.

b) I studied two hours for the test; as a result, I was pleased with my grade.

c) I studied two hours for the test, as a result I was pleased with my grade.

d) I studied two hours for the test, as a result, I was pleased with my grade.

13. My new apartment is in Manhattan but I work on Staten Island.

a) My new apartment is in Manhattan but, I work on Staten Island.

b) My new apartment is in Manhattan but I work on Staten Island.

c) My new apartment is in Manhattan, but I work on Staten Island.

d) My new apartment is in Manhattan; but I work on Staten Island.

14. My favorite movie is <u>The Color Purple</u> consequently I've watched it twelve times.

a) My favorite movie is <u>The Color Purple</u>, consequently I've watched it twelve times.

b) My favorite movie is <u>The Color Purple</u>; consequently, I've watched it twelve times.

c) My favorite movie is <u>The Color Purple</u>, consequently; I've watched it twelve times.

d) My favorite movie is <u>The Color Purple</u> consequently I've watched it twelve times.

15. I don't like going to the dentist thus I have missed two appointments.

a) I don't like going to the dentist thus I have missed two appointments.

b) I don't like going to the dentist; thus, I have missed two appointments.

c) I don't like going to the dentist, thus I have missed two appointments.

d) I don't like going to the dentist; thus I have missed two appointments.

Chapter Sixteen Test B

Beyond the Simple Sentence: Coordination

I. Combine the sentence pairs using the following three options:

1) a comma and a coordinating conjunction

2) a semicolon

3) a semicolon and a conjunctive adverb (with a comma if needed)

John telephoned the police.

Help arrived in thirty minutes.

1. Option 1._____

2. Option 2. _____

3. Option 3. _____

The bicycle was left in the driveway.

Mr. Johnson slammed on the brakes to avoid hitting it.

4. Option 1._____

5. Option 2._____

6. Option 3._____

II. Add a comma, or a semicolon, or a comma and a semicolon to the following sentences. Do not add, change, or delete any words.

7. Children can be taught many rules but they still require supervision.

8. The firemen were notified early therefore the blaze was quickly extinguished.

9. Television can be entertaining and educational it can also have negative effects.

10. Dark clouds formed overhead then the rain came down in torrents.

11. Jake wasn't our first choice nevertheless he did an incredible job.

12. I worked very hard on the project thus I was not surprised by the award I received.

13. The customers raced to the bargain table they grabbed all of the discount clothing.

14. The mice escaped from the box and one ran into the hallway.

15. A rainstorm delayed the parade however the children did not lose their enthusiasm.

16. Lasagna is my favorite dish I eat it once a week.

17. The ice had not frozen completely therefore the judges postponed the skating events.

18. She did not eat her breakfast nor did she eat her dinner.

19. I finished the project last night and I turned it in this morning.

20. Adam's car would not start so I gave him a ride to work.

Chapter Seventeen Test A
Avoiding Run-On Sentences and Comma Splices

Select the answer that corrects the comma splice or run-on sentence.

1. Marty dreamed of being a star, therefore he auditioned almost every week.

a) Marty dreamed of being a star, therefore, he auditioned almost every week.

b) Marty dreamed of being a star, therefore; he auditioned almost every week.

c) Marty dreamed of being a star therefore he auditioned almost every week.

d) Marty dreamed of being a star; therefore, he auditioned almost every week.

2. I love to play tennis I'm not very good at it.

a) I love to play tennis, I'm not very good at it.

b) I love to play tennis but, I'm not very good at it.

c) I love to play tennis, but I'm not very good at it.

d) I love to play tennis however I'm not very good at it.

3. Janet left fingerprints on the glass, the detectives were able to solve the crime.

a) Janet left fingerprints on the glass, consequently, the detectives were able to solve the crime.

b) Janet left fingerprints on the glass; consequently, the detectives were able to solve the crime.

c) Janet left fingerprints on the glass so the detectives were able to solve the crime.

d) Janet left fingerprints on the glass the detectives were able to solve the crime.

4. The scouts weren't prepared for the hike they were exhausted when they made camp.

a) The scouts weren't prepared for the hike, they were exhausted when they made camp.

b) The scouts weren't prepared for the hike; they were exhausted when they made camp.

c) The scouts weren't prepared for the hike so, they were exhausted when they made camp.

d) The scouts weren't prepared for the hike; so, they were exhausted when they made camp.

5. It's not easy to find a good job, many people take jobs they don't want.

a) It's not easy to find a good job, so many people take jobs they don't want.

b) It's not easy to find a good job, thus many people take jobs they don't want.

c) It's not easy to find a good job thus, many people take jobs they don't want.

d) It's not easy to find a good job so, many people take jobs they don't want.

6. We worked on the science project last night we hope to finish it soon.

a) We worked on the science project last night; and we hope to finish it soon.

b) We worked on the science project last night and, we hope to finish it soon.

c) We worked on the science project last night; we hope to finish it soon.

d) We worked on the science project last night and we hope to finish it soon.

7. The farmers stood in line all afternoon they wanted to get a good price for their crops.

a) The farmers stood in line all afternoon; they, wanted to get a good price for their crops.

b) The farmers stood in line all afternoon for, they wanted to get a good price for their crops.

c) The farmers stood in line all afternoon; for they wanted to get a good price for their crops.

d) The farmers stood in line all afternoon, for they wanted to get a good price for their crops.

8. We were married on Valentine's Day, it was a romantic ceremony.

a) We were married on Valentine's Day, it was a romantic ceremony.

b) We were married on Valentine's Day; it was a romantic ceremony.

c) We were married on Valentine's Day and, it was a romantic ceremony.

d) We were married on Valentine's Day; and it was a romantic ceremony.

9. I must be a genius I figured out how to register for classes with no complications.

a) I must be a genius, as a result, I figured out how to register for classes with no complications.

b) I must be a genius; as a result I figured out how to register for classes with no complications.

c) I must be a genius, as a result I figured out how to register for classes with no complications.

d) I must be a genius; as a result, I figured out how to register for classes with no complications.

10. The computers were on sale so I purchased a new laptop.

a) The computers were on sale, so I purchased a new laptop.

b) The computers were on sale so, I purchased a new laptop.

c) The computers were on sale; so I purchased a new laptop.

d) The computers were on sale; so, I purchased a new laptop.

11. Barbara wanted the promotion unfortunately she compromised her morals to get it.

a) Barbara wanted the promotion, unfortunately; she compromised her morals to get it.

b) Barbara wanted the promotion, unfortunately, she compromised her morals to get it.

c) Barbara wanted the promotion; unfortunately, she compromised her morals to get it.

d) Barbara wanted the promotion, unfortunately she compromised her morals to get it.

12. We only watched movies and drank soda, Saturday nights weren't exciting at our house.

a) We only watched movies and drank soda Saturday nights weren't exciting at our house.

b) We only watched movies and drank soda, Saturday nights weren't exciting at our house.

c) We only watched movies and drank soda; Saturday nights weren't exciting at our house.

d) We only watched movies and drank soda for Saturday nights weren't exciting at our house.

13. High heels hurt my feet but my new shoes look great with my dress.

a) High heels hurt my feet but, my new shoes look great with my dress.

b) High heels hurt my feet, but my new shoes look great with my dress.

c) High heels hurt my feet; but my new shoes look great with my dress.

d) High heels hurt my feet; but, my new shoes look great with my dress.

14. Jeff left Annette at the altar her mother vowed to get revenge.

a) Jeff left Annette at the altar, her mother vowed to get revenge.

b) Jeff left Annette at the altar; then her mother vowed to get revenge.

c) Jeff left Annette at the altar, then her mother vowed to get revenge.

d) Jeff left Annette at the altar, then, her mother vowed to get revenge.

15. The psychic predicted rain, it snowed all evening.

a) The psychic predicted rain it snowed all evening.

b) The psychic predicted rain but it snowed all evening.

c) The psychic predicted rain but, it snowed all evening.

d) The psychic predicted rain; however, it snowed all evening.

Chapter Seventeen Test B

Avoiding Run-On Sentences and Comma Splices

Correct each comma splice and run-on sentence using different methods.

Martha was married to George, she was in love with Arnold.

1. _____

2. _____

We ordered a seven-course meal we had only enough money for beverages.

3. _____

4. _____

Performing community service can be rewarding, it is a great opportunity to meet new people.

5. _____

6. _____

Ice cream can be high in calories yogurt is a healthy alternative.

7. _____

8. _____

I had a flat tire on the way to my interview, I arrived thirty minutes late.

9. _____

10. _____

Chapter Eighteen Test A
Beyond the Simple Sentence: Subordination

Determine if the sentence needs a comma. Select Yes or No.

1. Even though I am a registered voter I didn't go to the polls today.

a) Yes

b) No

2. I left home early because I wanted to get a good seat at the theater.

a) Yes

b) No

3. Chewing gum helped me to stop smoking since it was nicotine-flavored gum.

a) Yes

b) No

4. Unless I study all night I won't pass this test.

a) Yes

b) No

5. While I ate dinner I admired my new china.

a) Yes

b) No

6. When my date arrived I was still getting dressed.

a) Yes

b) No

7. I auditioned for the play as if I had a chance of getting the lead role.

a) Yes

b) No

8. You need to move your car before it is towed.

a) Yes

b) No

9. If you shampoo the rugs tonight they will be dry in the morning.

a) Yes

b) No

10. Debra will renew her license when she returns from vacation.

a) Yes

b) No

11. Since the movie started at nine we decided to shoot some pool first.

a) Yes

b) No

12. As I was getting out of the shower I slipped and fell on the tiles.

a) Yes

b) No

13. The speaker remained at the podium even though the audience was leaving.

a) Yes

b) No

14. After we left the museum we stopped at the library.

a) Yes

b) No

15. Employers are not pleased when employees misuse sick leave.

a) Yes

b) No

Chapter Eighteen Test B

Beyond the Simple Sentence: Subordination

I. **Combine the sentences using subordination. Begin the sentences with dependent clauses.**

Helen likes to give parties in her home.

Her guests never enjoy themselves.

1._____

2._____

II. **Combine the sentences using subordination. End the sentences with dependent clauses.**

3._____

4._____

III. **Add a comma to each sentence that needs one. Some sentences do not need a comma.**

5. Since I had driven all night I slept until noon.

6. Rita and Janet blushed because everyone was watching them.

7. Even though it was raining the children did not leave the pool.

8. After standing in line for hours I finally got my concert tickets.

9. The tree will be cut down unless the park officials get enough signatures on the petition.

10. Whenever the doorbell rings both dogs begin to bark.

11. I cleaned the entire house while you were sleeping.

12. The Kelleys sold their house when all of their kids moved away.

13. Before I was adopted my parents tried desperately to have a baby.

14. Everyone was having a good time until the neighbors started to complain about the noise.

15. When it is time to take a vacation planning is very important.

Avoiding Sentence Fragments

Label each group of words as fragment or sentence.

1. The man walking his puppy on the leash.

a) fragment

b) sentence

2. Jake wanted to vote in the upcoming election.

a) fragment

b) sentence

3. After the cab ride through town.

a) fragment

b) sentence

4. Without a chance to clean the house before the guests arrived.

a) fragment

b) sentence

5. Because it was our anniversary, we went out for dinner and dancing.

a) fragment

b) sentence

6. Although Wanda wanted a new dress for the party.

a) fragment

b) sentence

7. The soldiers returning from the war.

a) fragment

b) sentence

8. Faith Hill, my favorite singer, appeared on stage last night.

a) fragment

b) sentence

9. Turned into the worst night of my life.

a) fragment

b) sentence

10. Hoping to get into the sold-out concert.

a) fragment

b) sentence

11. Nail-biting is often an indicator of nervousness.

a) fragment

b) sentence

12. Behind the sofa are my hat and gloves.

a) fragment

b) sentence

13. Because of the cold weather and the forecast of more snow.

a) fragment

b) sentence

14. The butler invited our dinner guests into the living room for coffee.

a) fragment

b) sentence

15. Whenever I am depressed and need to lift my spirits.

a) fragment

b) sentence

Chapter Nineteen Test B

Avoiding Sentence Fragments

I. Put an S beside each complete sentence and an F beside each fragment.

1. ____ The men watching the basketball game.

2. ____ Since I didn't believe the fortune teller's prediction.

3. ____ In addition, Mary purchased beverages for the convention.

4. ____ After a long run, I take a long, soothing shower.

5. ____ For example, a house with a basement and an attic.

6. ____ Expecting the judges to arrive at any minute.

7. ____ While the baby napped, Martha relaxed on the couch.

8. ____ Especially the one with the shiny surface.

9. ____ In the back of the closet is a pair of old shoes.

10. ____ Around the corner near the end of the street.

11. ____ Although the furniture did not arrive on time.

12. ____ The factory worker with the contracts in his hand.

13. ____ Samantha watched while the building collapsed.

14. ____ The winner to be announced after the election.

15. ____ The pianist upset by the noisy audience.

II. Correct each sentence fragment in the most appropriate way.

16. After losing their map in the woods. The stranded campers radioed for help.

17. The actor walking slowly across the stage.

18. I decided to go home early. Even though I had promised to stay.

19. Whenever she baby-sits small children. Nikki brings toys and refreshments.

20. There was no way to repair the broken china. Shattered on the hard floor.

Chapter Twenty Test A
Using Parallelism in Sentences

Select the answer with parallel structure.

1. I spent Saturday afternoon cleaning the bathroom, I cooked, and also washed dishes.

a) I spent Saturday afternoon cleaning the bathroom, cooking, and I washed the dishes.

b) I spent Saturday afternoon cleaning, and I cooked dinner and washed the dishes.

c) I spent Saturday afternoon cleaning the bathroom, cooking dinner, and washing dishes.

d) I used Saturday afternoon to clean the bathroom, to cook dinner, and wash dishes.

2. Three characteristics of a good friend are giving support, compassion, and being kind.

a) Three characteristics of a good friend are giving support, giving compassion, and kindness.

b) Three characteristics of a good friend are support, compassion, and kindness.

c) Three characteristics of a good friend are being supportive, showing compassion, and kindness.

d) Three characteristics of a good friend are giving support, compassion, and showing kindness.

3. The teen's biggest fears were acne, being alone, and speaking in front of others.

a) The teen's biggest fears were acne, loneliness, and public speaking.

b) The teen's biggest fears were getting acne, being alone, and public speaking.

c) The teen's biggest fears were acne, being alone, and public speaking.

d) The teen's biggest fears were acne, loneliness, and speaking in front of others.

4. When you get to the cabin, you must check the cupboards for food, you need to start the fire, and make sure the pipes aren't frozen.

a) When you get to the cabin, you must check the cupboards, start the fire, and pipes must be checked.

b) When you get to the cabin, your job is checking the cupboards for food, starting a fire, and you have to make sure the pipes aren't frozen.

c) When you get to the cabin, you must find food, start the fire, and you need to check for frozen pipes.

d) When you get to the cabin, you must check for food, start the fire, and check for frozen pipes.

5. The cat's low weight, its broken claws, and the fact that its fur was matted indicated the animal was being neglected.

a) The cat's low weight, the claws were broken, and the matted fur indicated the animal was being neglected.

b) The cat has low weight, and the claws are broken and the matted fur indicated the animal was being neglected.

c) The cat's low weight, broken claws, and matted fur indicated the animal was being neglected.

d) The cat's low weight, broken claws, and its fur was matted which indicated the animal was being neglected.

6. We searched for the lost keys in the yard, the toy box, and we looked in my purse.

a) We searched for the lost keys in the yard, and we looked in the toy box, and my purse.

b) We searched for the lost keys in the yard, the toy box, and looked in my purse.

c) We searched for the lost keys in the yard, the toy box, and inside my purse.

d) We searched for the lost keys in the yard, inside the toy box, and in my purse.

7. I thought the play was funny, it taught a lesson, and it was entertaining.

a) I thought the play was funny, educational, and entertaining.

b) I thought the play was funny, taught a lesson, and was entertaining.

c) I thought the play was funny, taught a lesson, and entertained.

d) I thought the play was funny, taught lessons, and was entertaining.

8. Our day at the spa included getting manicures, we had facials, and we enjoyed a massage.

a) Our day at the spa included getting manicures, facials, and we enjoyed massages.

b) Our day at the spa included manicures, facials, and massages.

c) Our day at the spa included getting our nails manicured, facials, and body massages.

d) Our day at the spa included manicures, we had facials, and got massages.

9. Picking up the children, make afternoon snacks, and organizing outdoor activities are my jobs at the daycare center.

a) Picking up the children, the afternoon snacks, and organizing outdoor activities are my jobs at the daycare center.

b) To pick up the children, make afternoon snacks, and organizing the outdoor activities are my jobs at the daycare center.

c) Picking up the children, making afternoon snacks, and organizing outdoor activities are my jobs at the daycare center.

d) My jobs at the daycare are pick up the children, make afternoon snacks, and organizing outdoor activities.

10. Routine locker checks at high schools expose illegal weapons, some kids hide drugs, and there are pictures of friends.

a) Routine locker checks at high schools expose illegal weapons, hidden drugs, and some kids have pictures.

b) Routine locker checks at high schools expose illegal weapons, hidden drugs, and there are some pictures of friends.

c) Routine locker checks at high schools expose guns, some drugs, and they hang pictures of friends.

d) Routine locker checks at high schools expose illegal weapons, drugs, and pictures.

11. At the party, the clown entertained the kids with magic tricks, he told jokes, and he made balloon animals.

a) At the party, the clown entertained the kids with magic tricks, he told jokes, and balloon animals.

b) At the party, the clown entertained the kids with magic tricks, jokes, and he made balloon animals.

c) At the party, the clown performed magic tricks, told jokes, and made balloon animals.

d) At the party, the clown entertained the kids by performing magic tricks, he told jokes, and made balloon animals.

12. The concert will begin at nine; midnight is when it will be ending.

a) The concert begins at nine; it ends at midnight.

b) The concert begins at nine; at midnight it will be ending.

c) The concert will begin at nine; at midnight is the end.

d) The concert will begin at nine, ending at midnight.

13. Jenna will succeed in life because of her dedication, she respects herself, and she has ambition.

a) Jenna will succeed in life because of dedication, she respects herself, and ambition.

b) Jenna will succeed in life because of her dedication, self-respect, and ambition.

c) Jenna will succeed in life because she is dedicated, she respects herself, and ambition.

d) Jenna will succeed in life because of dedication, she respects herself, and she has ambition.

14. The plumber unclogged the drain, the pipes had to be flushed, and he fixed the garbage disposal.

a) The plumber unclogged the drain, the pipes were flushed, and the garbage disposal was fixed.

b) The plumber unclogged the drain, flushed the pipes, and fixed the garbage disposal.

c) The plumber unclogged the drain, flushed the pipes, and fixed the garbage disposal.

d) The plumber unclogged the drain, flushed the pipes, and he fixed the garbage disposal.

15. Exercising daily strengthens the bones, it boosts energy levels, and people lose weight.

a) Exercising daily makes the bones stronger, energy levels rise, and people lose weight.

b) Exercising daily strengthens bones, boosts energy, and weight is lost.

c) Exercising daily strengthens bones, boosts energy levels, and promotes weight loss.

d) Exercising daily strengthens the bones, boosts energy levels, and it helps people lose weight.

Chapter Twenty Test B
Using Parallelism in Sentences

I. Revise the following sentences so that they have parallel structure.

1. My new job includes watering the plants, the floors have to be cleaned, and filing documents.

2. The meeting began at ten; twelve was the time it ended.

3. The millionaire likes fast cars, women who are pretty, and houses that are large.

4. The restaurant was crowded, dirty, and the food cost too much.

5. During the summer, we enjoy hiking, going fishing, and to hunt.

6. It is easier to shop for vegetables than planting a garden.

7. The new office manager is loud, not very smart, and rude.

8. The actress has appeared in movies and television.

9. Bob likes reading, to write, and he is a good teacher.

10. The lecture was entertaining, time consuming, and it taught me new things.

II. Combine each cluster of sentences into one sentence that contains parallel structure.

11. Our new house has many rooms.

    The large windows flood the house with light.

    The price fit our budget.

12. We need to decrease our phone bill.

    Our electric bill must be lowered also.

    Too much money is wasted on groceries that no one eats.

13. Potted plants were placed near the patio doors.

    Some were on the kitchen counter.

    There were several plants in the bathroom.

14. Television commercials entice consumers to buy products.

    Advertisements can often be deceptive.

    Some commercials rely upon humor to sell products.

Chapter Twenty-One Test A
Using Adjectives and Adverbs

Select the correct adjective or adverb.

1. You did _____ on the test.
   a) good
   b) bad
   c) worse
   d) well

2. My sister Janet is _____ than my brother.
   a) more older
   b) older
   c) oldest
   d) most older

3. This book is _____ than the other book I read.
   a) more interesting
   b) more good
   c) most better
   d) most interesting

4. Of the three men, Jake is the _____.
   a) handsomest
   b) handsomer
   c) more handsome
   d) most handsome

5. I walked _____ to the catch the bus.
   a) more quick
   b) quick
   c) quickly
   d) quicker

6. The dog ate its food _____.

a) greedy

b) greedily

c) more greedy

d) quick

7. In ballet class, she dances _____.

a) gracefully

b) graceful

c) awkward

d) slow

8. I want to date someone _____ than Ted.

a) most tall

b) taller

c) more taller

d) most taller

9. The sailor is _____ than the rest of his crew.

a) more skilled

b) skillfully

c) skillful

d) most skilled

10. We prepared three dishes for dinner; the spaghetti was the _____ of the three.

a) more healthy

b) worse

c) better

d) best

11. My husband is _____ than his brother.

a) wealthier

b) most wealthier

c) more wealthier

d) more poor

12. Of the four subjects I took this semester, Spanish was the _____.

a) more difficult

b) most difficult

c) easier

d) more easier

13. I want a _____ old classic car.

a) real

b) most

c) very

d) more

14. The thief was _____ sorry for his crime.

a) sincerely

b) sure

c) more

d) most

15. The architect _____ packed her plans to present to the committee.

a) real careful

b) careful

c) more carefully

d) carefully

Chapter Twenty-One Test B
Using Adjectives and Adverbs

I. Underline each adjective in the following sentences.

1. Shannon is the best student in class.

2. I was very happy to find my lost puppy.

3. Buying the fur coat was a bad choice.

4. Cold winter nights make me wish for springtime.

5. The cautious burglar slowly entered the broken window.

6. The large, green cabin was nestled in the dark woods.

7. Dirty laundry should be washed immediately.

8. The fat, little girl in the blue sweater looks hungry.

9. The old turtle slowly crossed the busy intersection.

10. The milk tastes spoiled.

II. Underline each adverb in the following sentences.

11. Mike crossed the dilapidated bridge very carefully.

12. The huge dog growled angrily at the salesman.

13. The children behaved badly during the concert.

14. You did well on the grammar test.

15. I rarely visit my old neighborhood.

16. Susan practices yoga often.

17. We can barely afford to pay our rent.

18. The frantic woman desperately searched for her lost child.

19. Mom drives slowly and cautiously when it is raining.

20. I have successfully completed my studies.

III. Correct errors in the use of adjectives and adverbs.

When I was a young, college student, I decided to major in English instead of biology. My decision was not made quick. I knew that I had not done good in English in high school. I was a more better biology student, so English was the worst choice. However, I did not choose bad. I studied hard and made well grades.

Chapter Twenty-Two Test A
Correcting Problems with Modifiers

Select the answer that corrects the modifier errors.

1. Without checking the cost, the sequined wedding gown on the mannequin was purchased.

   a) Without checking the cost, a purchase of the sequined wedding gown on the mannequin was made.

   b) Without checking the cost, Marsha purchased the sequined wedding gown on the mannequin.

   c) Marsha purchased the sequined wedding gown without checking the cost on the mannequin.

   d) On the mannequin, Marsha purchased the sequined wedding gown without checking the cost.

2. Wynona went to the governor's ball wearing a red dress with purple feathers.

   a) With purple feathers, Wynona went to the governor's ball wearing a red dress.

   b) Wearing a red dress, Wynona went to the governor's ball with purple feathers.

   c) Wearing a red dress with purple feathers, Wynona went to the governor's ball.

   d) With purple feathers, Wynona, wearing a red dress, went to the governor's ball.

3. At the age of six, my mother was promoted to full partner in her law firm.

   a) When I was six, my mother was promoted to full partner in her law firm.

   b) At the age of six in her law firm, my mother was promoted to full partner.

   c) In her law firm when I was at the age of six, my mother was promoted to full partner.

   d) My mother was promoted to full partner in her law firm at the age of six.

4. Struggling to keep his head above water, the rescuers in the helicopter spotted the drowning man.

   a) The rescuers spotted the drowning man in the helicopter struggling to keep his head above water.

   b) Struggling to keep his head above water in the helicopter, the rescuers spotted the drowning man.

   c) Struggling, the rescuers in the helicopter spotted the drowning man.

   d) The rescuers in the helicopter spotted the drowning man in the water struggling to keep his head above water.

5. While making plans for vacation, the phone in the den rang.

a) The phone in the den rang while making plans for vacation.

b) While the family was making plans for vacation, the phone rang.

c) The phone rang while making plans for vacation in the den.

d) In the den, the phone rang while making plans for vacation.

6. Driving over rugged terrain, the supplies in the back of the jeep fell to the floor.

a) As the campers were driving over rugged terrain, the supplies in the back of the jeep fell to the floor.

b) The supplies in the back of the jeep fell to the floor while driving over rugged terrain.

c) In the back of the jeep, the supplies fell to the floor while driving over rugged terrain.

d) The supplies fell to the floor in the back of the jeep while driving over rugged terrain.

7. Jeff slowly opened the door, afraid of seeing his angry girlfriend.

a) Afraid, Jeff opened the door seeing his angry girlfriend.

b) Jeff opened the door, afraid of seeing his angry girlfriend slowly.

c) Afraid of seeing his angry girlfriend, Jeff slowly opened the door.

d) Jeff opened the door afraid of his angry girlfriend.

8. While attempting to fax the documents, the customer's number was misdialed.

a) The customer's number was misdialed while attempting to fax the documents.

b) While the secretary was attempting to fax the documents, the customer's number was misdialed.

c) Faxing the document, the customer's number was misdialed.

d) The customer's number, while attempting to fax the documents, was misdialed.

9. The puppy chewed a hole in the shoes that we selected at the pound.

a) The puppy that we selected at the pound chewed a hole in the shoes.

b) On the shoes, the puppy that we selected at the pound chewed a hole.

c) The puppy that we selected chewed a hole in the shoes at the pound.

d) In the shoes that we selected at the pound, the puppy chewed a hole.

10. Tired and thirsty after the hike, the sight of the house was welcomed.

a) We welcomed the sight of the house, tired and thirsty.

b) Tired and thirsty, the sight of the house after the hike was welcomed.

c) Tired and thirsty after the hike, the scouts welcomed the sight of the house.

d) The sight of the house was welcomed after the hike.

11. After purchasing a new computer with a modem, the Internet would be accessible.

a) The Internet would be accessible after purchasing a new computer with a modem.

b) With a modem, the Internet would be accessible after purchasing a new computer.

c) With a modem after purchasing a new computer, the Internet would be accessible.

d) After John purchased a new computer with a modem, the Internet was accessible to him.

12. The flowers decorated the foyer cut fresh from the garden.

a) Cut fresh from the garden, the flowers decorated the foyer.

b) They decorated the foyer, cut fresh from the garden.

c) The flowers decorated the foyer after being cut fresh from the garden.

d) Decorating the foyer cut fresh from the garden were the flowers.

13. The dentist told me to floss my teeth during my visit with a stern look.

a) During my visit with a stern look, the dentist told me to floss my teeth.

b) During my visit, the dentist told me to floss my teeth with a stern look.

c) During my visit, the dentist, with a stern look, told me to floss my teeth.

d) The dentist, with a stern look, told me to floss my teeth during my visit.

14. Destroyed by fire, we searched for valuables in the ashes.

a) We searched for valuables in the ashes destroyed by fire.

b) After the museum was destroyed by fire, we searched for valuables in the ashes.

c) Destroyed by fire we searched the ashes for valuables.

d) We searched in the ashes destroyed by the fire.

15. The volunteers painted the building dressed in casual clothes for two hours.

a) Dressed in casual clothes, the volunteers painted the building for two hours.

b) For two hours, the volunteers painted the building dressed in casual clothes.

c) Dressed in casual clothes, the building was painted for two hours.

d) The volunteers painted the building in casual clothes for two hours.

Chapter Twenty-Two Test B

Correcting Problems with Modifiers

Some of the following sentences contain misplaced or dangling modifier errors. Correct them by moving, adding, changing or removing words. Label correct sentences OK.

1. Jenny stepped on a large snake weeding in her garden.

2. We only want to watch cartoons on television.

3. The fish, exhausted and injured, struggled to free itself from the hook.

4. Tangled and dirty, my mother spent two hours styling my hair.

5. Running was difficult after tripping and falling on the jogging path.

6. The winner returned to her chair smiling jubilantly.

7. Driving through the country, wild flowers scented the air.

8. Afraid of being burned by the sun, Tammy crouched under the umbrella.

9. The clerk gave a sundae to the child with a cherry on top.

10. After six hours of studying, the test was not difficult.

11. Exhausted after working a double shift, the bed was warm and soothing.

12. Disturbed by the dancers, the lamp tipped nearly over.

13. Antonio was ready for the interview dressed in a new suit.

14. Samantha gave her father a watch with a gold band.

15. We took the dog to the vet with fleas.

Chapter Twenty-Three Test A

Using Verbs Correctly

Select the correct verb.

1. A good son _____ his mother almost every day.

a) call

b) help

c) see

d) calls

2. Yesterday, the police officer _____ eight speeders.

a) arrest

b) arrested

c) stop

d) upsets

3. Now, I _____ to my teacher.

a) listens

b) listened

c) am listening

d) be listening

4. The janitor _____ the only person left in the room.

a) is

b) are

c) were

d) be

5. On Thanksgiving, we always _____ a large meal.

a) eats

b) eating

c) eaten

d) eat

6. The sergeant of the company _____ her soldiers to shoot rifles.

a) teaching

b) were teaching

c) taught

d) teach

7. The class _____ a retirement party for Dr. James.

a) be planning

b) are planning

c) was planning

d) plan

8. The fashionable women _____ designer clothing to the luncheon.

a) wore

b) wears

c) is wearing

d) was wearing

9. Last night, my dog _____ for an hour.

a) is howling

b) howl

c) howls

d) howled

10. In the past, we _____ several historic sites.

a) visit

b) had visited

c) visits

d) are visiting

11. I _____ the paperwork before I left for the day.

a) done

b) did

c) finish

d) finishes

12. Roberto _____ his mother for lunch money each day.

a) asking

b) ask

c) asks

d) been asking

13. A yellow Volkswagen Beetle _____ the car I want.

a) be

b) were

c) are

d) is

14. I _____ interested in purchasing a new stereo.

a) am

b) are

c) be

d) were

15. The small town _____ included on the state map.

a) were

b) was

c) are

d) be

Chapter Twenty-Three Test B
Using Verbs Correctly

Choose the correct form of the verb in each sentence.

1. Bacon (contain / contains) a large number of calories.

2. I (was / were) shocked by the robbery.

3. Watching television (is / are) a popular pastime.

4. Near the corner (is / are) a fire hydrant.

5. The letter was (wrote / written) by the president of the club.

6. You (has / have) to make a decision soon.

7. Marla (want / wants) the doll with the shiny hair.

8. Last night, John (call / called) to get directions to my house.

9. Louisa (make / made) a mess in the kitchen.

10. He (do / does) not know the answer.

11. Behind the statue (stand / stands) a huge fountain.

12. It (don't / doesn't) matter which way we go.

13. The tourists (is / are) boarding the bus.

14. Justin should have (tell / told) his mother about the fight.

15. At midday, the sun (shine / shines) on the lake.

16. I (listen / listens) to music while I study.

17. Ronald (walk / walks) Melissa to class each day.

18. I have (saw / seen) many accidents at this intersection.

19. This food (taste / tastes) spoiled.

20. Yesterday, Julia (tell / told) me about her new business venture.

Chapter Twenty-Four Test A
Making Subjects and Verbs Agree

Select the correct verb.

1. Neither the players nor the coach _____ the final score.

a) knows

b) know

2. The herd _____ around the lake after the rain ends.

a) gathers

b) gather

3. All members of the team _____ expected to attend practice each day.

a) is

b) are

4. Everyone in the building _____ ready to go home.

a) is

b) are

5. Ted and his children _____ supposed to visit us during Christmas vacation.

a) is

b) are

6. There _____ a statue of George Washington and a fountain in the square.

a) is

b) are

7. Marty or his friends _____ decided to picket a local business.

a) has

b) have

8. _____ your sister and brother plan to attend the debate tonight?

a) Do

b) Does

9. A box of apples _____ more than a box of oranges.

a) costs

b) cost

10. The jury _____ fighting about the verdict.

a) is

b) are

11. Mr. Jenson, along with his brothers, _____ responsible for cleaning the conference room after the meeting.

a) is

b) are

12. Here _____ your birth certificate and your driver's license.

a) is

b) are

13. In the room behind the door _____ my puppy.

a) is

b) are

14. Not only the teacher but also the students _____ ready for spring break.

a) is

b) are

15. Each person on the committee _____ supposed to participate in the telethon.

a) was

b) were

Chapter Twenty-Four Test B

Making Subjects and Verbs Agree

Circle the correct verb in parentheses in each sentence below.

1. Everyone in class (need / needs) to study.

2. Not only Charles but also his parents (eat / eats) dinner at nine.

3. The herd of cattle (drink / drinks) water from the lake in the pasture.

4. After school, Vivian and I (walk / walks) to the library.

5. Near the center of town (is / are) a statue of a horse and rider.

6. Pigeons (flock / flocks) to gather food left by the tourists.

7. There (is / are) chickens and pigs on my uncle's farm.

8. Either roses or tulips (is / are) planted in the fall.

9. Neither of the skaters (cross / crosses) the finish line in time.

10. Martin, as well as Ben, (apply / applies) for the job at the car wash.

11. Someone from the shop (take / takes) the deposit to the bank at closing time.

12. The child with the soft voice and the sad face (seem / seems) unhappy.

13. (Do / Does) your mother and father give you a weekly allowance?

14. The company (hire / hires) new employees before the Labor Day holiday.

15. The athletes on the team (practices / practice) on the field after school.

16. My purse, along with my shoes, (match / matches) my new dress.

17. Either Stephanie or her neighbors (stay / stays) at home during the holidays.

18. Each of the winners (receives / receive) a trophy and a scholarship.

19. Where (is / are) the list of groceries?

20. Neither the electricity nor the plumbing (works / work) properly in the old house.

Chapter Twenty-Five Test A
Using Pronouns Correctly: Agreement and Reference

Select the correct pronoun.

1. The employees were pleased with the company because _____ gave annual pay raises.

a) it

b) they

2. Everyone in the class took _____ test on pronouns.

a) his

b) his or her

3. While playing with the kites, the children lost _____ dog in the park.

a) his or her

b) their

4. Jasmine and Sarah played basketball because _____ wanted to travel with the team.

a) they

b) she

5. Many people invest in mutual funds hoping to increase _____ money.

a) his or her

b) their

6. I left the Chess Club since _____ required too much of my time.

a) it

b) they

7. Steven and Jeff thought _____ project would win an award in the science fair.

a) his

b) their

8. The umpires went on strike, for _____ wanted larger salaries and more benefits.

a) he

b) they

9. The trapped lion paced in _____ cage.

a) its

b) their

10. The family decorated _____ tree on Christmas Eve.

a) its

b) their

11. Everybody at the canceled concert demanded that _____ money be refunded.

a) their

b) his or her

12. One of the players on the soccer team twisted _____ ankle.

a) their

b) her

13. Most parents feel _____ aren't too strict with their children.

a) he

b) they

14. The team will play _____ first game on Saturday.

a) its

b) their

15. Somebody left _____ calculus notes in the classroom.

a) their

b) his or her

Chapter Twenty-Five Test B
Using Pronouns Correctly: Agreement and Reference

I.   Circle the correct pronoun in the parentheses in each sentence.

1. Everyone should select (her / their) career carefully.

2. Neither of the men wanted (his / their) picture in the paper.

3. The soldiers demonstrated (his / their) survival skills in the desert.

4. Melanie and Jessica waited patiently for (her / their) chance to perform.

5. The jury gave (its / their) verdict after hours of deliberation.

6. The audience demonstrated (its / their) satisfaction by clapping frantically.

7. One of the boys left (his / their) glove on the field.

8. The congressmen expected harsh criticism from (his / their) constituents.

9. Most of the people in the community donated (her / their) time to help with the raffle.

10. The choir members practiced for (its / their) spring recital.

II. Correct problems with pronoun reference.

11. Graffiti covered most of the wall; it had to be removed.

12. At the daycare center, they charge a weekly fee.

13. Randa told Charlotte that she had to speak at the convention.

14. I received a raise at my job which pleased me.

15. Take the rug off the floor and wash it.

16. When I accidentally hit the car, he threatened me.

17. Philip and Christopher left the party in his car.

18. My mother and my aunt went to the spa; she enjoyed the massage.

19. The child kicked the dog, which angered his mother.

20. The butcher removed meat from the box and put it in the garbage can.

Chapter Twenty-Six Test A
Using Pronouns Correctly: Consistency and Case

Select the correct pronoun.

1. _____ complained to the police about the nosy neighbors.

a) He

b) Him

2. My mother warned me not to go on a date with _____.

a) he

b) him

3. _____ should have known about the errors in the report.

a) They

b) Them

4. The money in the envelope was a present for _____.

a) me

b) myself

5. Aunt Rosie knitted _____ a sweater with matching gloves.

a) he

b) him

6. Christy runs faster than _____.

a) she

b) her

7. After dinner, Casey and _____ will do our homework.

a) I

b) me

8. The detectives and _____ gathered evidence after the robbery.

a) us

b) we

9. Your voice is clearer than _____.

a) him

b) his

10. I spent a week reading _____ new murder mystery.

a) she

b) her

11. The coach and _____ voted on a new color for the uniforms.

a) we

b) us

12. Veronica and _____ wore identical gowns to the debutante ball.

a) I

b) me

13. I tried to reach _____ by phone last night.

a) they

b) them

14. The committee chair told _____ to prepare a budget before the new fiscal year.

a) we

b) us

15. The stray made _____ home in an abandoned building.

a) its

b) it's

Chapter Twenty-six Test B

Using Pronouns Correctly: Consistency and Case

I. Correct errors in pronoun consistency.

1. Every time I date Jacob, he makes you pay for dinner.

2. We need to be careful with our money; it's easy to exceed your budget.

3. Ramond loves to fish at the lake because you can catch large trout there.

4. The interior decorators will get more customers if you keep prices low.

5. Late at night, I don't answer my phone; the caller always upsets you.

6. I enjoy vacationing in Europe since you get to meet many interesting people.

7. She refused to cross the picket line because you had to respect the protesters' wishes.

8. As children, we waited anxiously for the store to open, for you knew you would get some candy.

9. You could tell it was autumn when we saw the falling leaves.

10. I hate to take my car to that garage because the mechanic tries to take advantage of you.

II. Circle the correct pronoun in parentheses in each sentence.

11. Jeremy gave Emma and (I / me) a tour of the museum.

12. Between you and (I / me), I don't think Andrew should be trusted with the money.

13. The florist and (we / us) delivered the bouquets for the wedding.

14. My best friend and (I / Me) promised to stay in touch after college.

15. The criminal's prison sentence upset his mother more than it upset (he / him).

16. Rachel is a more compassionate person than (her / she).

17. The dog wagged (its / it's) tail when the children arrived.

18. Mr. Rivers and (them / they) will select a guest speaker for the program.

19. My daughters and (me / I) enjoy Christmas shopping.

20. The plumber overcharged (us / we) for the repairs.

21. The party was a surprise for Sabrina and (myself / me).

22. Brandon offered the employees and (we / us) discount movie tickets.

23. Since I began my new job, I make more money than (him / he).

24. The race ended in a tie between Christina and (me / I).

25. To save money, Carlos and (she / her) carpool to work.

I.   Select the answer with correct punctuation.

1. Kayla asked Dr Ramirez if he was a surgeon

a) Kayla asked Dr Ramirez if he was a surgeon?

b) Kayla asked Dr Ramirez if he was a surgeon.

c) Kayla asked Dr. Ramirez if he was a surgeon.

d) Kayla asked Dr. Ramirez if he was a surgeon?

2. Mr and Mrs Johnson were upset when Jeff asked to stay out late

a) Mr. and Mrs. Johnson were upset when Jeff asked to stay out late?

b) Mr. and Mrs. Johnson were upset when Jeff asked to stay out late.

c) Mr. and Mrs Johnson were upset when Jeff asked to stay out late?

d) Mr and Mrs. Johnson were upset when Jeff asked to stay out late.

3. Did the movie start at 10 pm

a)   Did the movie start at 10 p.m..

b   Did the movie start at 10 p.m.

c)   Did the movie start at 10 pm.?

d)   Did the movie start at 10 p.m.?

II. Select the answer that states how the comma is used in the sentence.

4.   Danielle purchased a comb, a purse, and a scarf.

a) lister

b) linker

c) introducer

d) inserter

5. Anthony Rivers, the cheapest man in town, refused to donate to any charities.

a) lister

b) linker

c) introducer

d) inserter

6. I will sit with you during the play, or I will see you at intermission.

a) lister

b) linker

c) introducer

d) inserter

III. Select the punctuation mark needed in each sentence.

The dogs collar was a gift from Jess and Thomas.

e) dog's

f) was'

g) Jess'

h) Thomas'

7. The decorators needed a months notice to remodel his offices.

a) decorator's

b) month's

c) his'

d) office's

8. Lucas put the lens in someones glasses.

a) Lucas'

b) lens'

c) someone's

d) glasses'

9. In his history class, Jess made two As.

a) his'

b) class'

c) Jess'

d) A's

10. The star player was injured our chances of winning vanished.

a) semicolon

b) colon

11. My office was filthy papers littered the floor, books covered the desk, and dust covered the shelves.

a) semicolon

b) colon

12. I purchased the supplies for the trip snacks, batteries, clothes, and tents.

a) semicolon

b) colon

14. My car is broken therefore, I have to ride the bus this week.

a) semicolon

b) colon

15. The governor assessed the damage "Our town has been devastated by the flood. Every major building was destroyed, but we can rebuild."

a) semicolon

b) colon

Chapter Twenty-Seven Test B
Punctuation: The Basics

Add the missing punctuation in each sentence.

1. Mr and Mrs Smith asked their lawyer to prepare divorce papers

2. Dr Jackson received his MD last year

3. Why did Ms Williams leave church in the middle of service

4. Miss Johnson is working on a BA in mathematics

5. Did Mr Chavez ask Mrs Smith about volunteering at the fair

6. Jack Pembroke, Jr is nothing like his father, Jack Pembroke, Sr

7. The 8 am sessions at the gym have been postponed

8. I went to work at 6 am; I left at 5 pm

9. Mrs Chung asked if Dr Parker was teaching at the university in the fall

10. The preacher married Mr and Mrs Walter Barker

Chapter Twenty-Eight Test A

Spelling

Select the misspelled word in each sentence.

1. The bruise on my leg was begining to swell, so my doctor recommended medicine.

a) bruise

b) begining

c) recommended

d) medicine

2. Unfortunatly, my fourteen-year guarantee expired on Wednesday.

a) Unfortunatly

b) fourteen

c) guarantee

d) Wednesday

3. The hotel on Jefferson Avenue can accomodate a business conference or committee activity.

a) Avenue

b) accomodate

c) business

d) committee

4. It is not necessary to iron the hankerchief before the marriage ceremony.

a) necessary

b) iron

c) hankerchief

d) marriage

5. Can I persuade you to provide guidance for forty maintanance workers?

a) persuade

b) guidance

c) forty

d) maintanance

6. If possible, don't imterupt the doctor while he writes a prescription.

a) possible

b) imterupt

c) doctor

d) prescription

7. I eat alot of cereal when I am studying after ten o'clock.

a) alot

b) cereal

c) studying

d) o'clock

8. I exercise so I can stay physically fit; but permenent weight loss is hard to maintain.

a) exercise

b) physically

c) permenent

d) maintain

9. It is fascinating to watch Bryan tap his forhead when he is trying to guess the answer to a problem in mathematics.

a) fascinating

b) forhead

c) guess

d) mathematics

10. There is no fundamental guarantee that we can recognise true happiness.

a) fundamental

b) guarantee

c) recognise

d) happiness

11. The professor offered words of encouragment to the grateful athlete.

a) professor

b) encouragment

c) grateful

d) athlete

12. An American sodier performed illegal activities because he lacked discipline.

a) American

b) sodier

c) illegal

d) discipline

13. The heroes are eligible for awards, so they expect an iland vacation.

a) heroes

b) eligible

c) expect

d) iland

14. My friend and neighbor happens to be a profesor of psychology.

a) friend

b) neighbor

c) profesor

d) psychology

15. The new millenium was an exciting and mysterious event for the secretary.

a) millenium

b) exciting

c) mysterious

d) secretary

I.   Combine the following words and endings.

1. quit + er

2. fly + es

3. beauty + ful

4. defense + ive

5. sure + ly

6. shaky + er

7. church + es

8. win + ing

9. potato + es

10. place + ment

II. Apply the rules for using *ie* or *ei* in the following words.

11. h _ _ ght

12. f _ _ nd

13. bel _ _ ve

14. fr _ _ ght

15. perc _ _ ve

III. Circle the correct word in parentheses in each sentence below.

16. (Every time / Everytime) I ask Kyle for a favor, he refuses.

17. Randall does not live here (anymore / any more).

18. (Even though / Eventhough) the sofa was blue, it clashed with the carpets.

19. The den is (downstairs / down stairs), and the (bedroom / bed room) is upstairs.

20. I was (already / all ready) to deliver my speech two days before the convention started.

21. Sonja invited (everyone / every one) of her friends to the awards banquet.

22. My cousin attended (highschool / high school) in a (nearby / near by) town.

23. The leader of the protest movement stood (a part / apart) from the crowd.

24. The (bookkeeper / book keeper) made copies of the company's tax statements.

25. I sweat (alot / a lot) after aerobics class.

Chapter Twenty–Nine Test A
Words That Sound Alike/Look Alike

Select the correct word for each sentence.

1. The preacher stood before the couple at the _____ .

   a) alter

   b) altar

2. I didn't mean to _____ the glass when I put it in the sink.

   a) brake

   b) break

3. It is hard to _____ when everyone is talking.

   a) hear

   b) here

4. The _____ material on the sofa scratched my arm.

   a) course

   b) coarse

5. The usher directed us down the _____ by waving his flashlight.

   a) aisle

   b) isle

6. The _____ reason for the test is to assess your skills.

   a) principle

   b) principal

7. We checked the construction _____ for missing tools.

   a) cite

   b) site

8. _____ the best detectives on the squad.

a) They're

b) Their

9. I happen to be the _____ survivor.

a) soul

b) sole

10. It is fashionable to wear the sash around your _____.

a) waist

b) waste

11. I purchased _____ decorated with flowers and birds.

a) stationary

b) stationery

12. It is easy to _____ your child in a crowded department store.

a) loose

b) lose

13. My sister has the _____ of a saint.

a) patience

b) patients

14. Each of Aesop's fables has a _____.

a) morale

b) moral

15. In _____ years, the administrators conducted monthly drug screenings.

a) past

b) passed

Chapter Twenty–Nine Test B
Words That Sound Alike/Look Alike

Circle the correct word in parentheses in each sentence below.

1. Raleigh, the (capitol / capital) of North Carolina, is (farther / further) down the highway.

2. She is (to / too / two) busy to (wait / weight) in a long line.

3. (Your / You're) the (right / write) person for the job.

4. The (plane / plain) landed at a designated (cite / site/ sight) near the arena.

5. The runner was (quite / quit / quiet) excited when he (past / passed) his opponent on the track.

6. This (steak / stake) tastes better (than / then) the one I ate last night.

7. The child's (cloths / clothes / close) are made from a (coarse / course) fabric.

8. We (new / knew) that cab (fare / fair) would be costly.

9. Please do not (waste / waist) the (stationary / stationery) by writing useless notes.

10. (Its / It's) always fun to (hear / here) from old acquaintances.

11. The club took (presents / presence) to the (patience / patients) at the county hospital.

12. The bachelor (wind / wined / whined) and dined his date (thorough / through / threw) the night.

13. The pastor read the scripture (allowed / aloud) from the (alter / altar).

14. My mother will (by / buy) more (cereal / serial) when she goes to the market.

15. I have a (moral / morale) obligation to be a responsible (women / woman).

16. (Whether / Weather) you like it or not, (were / we're / where) getting married.

17. (Would / Wood) you like cake or ice cream for (dessert / desert)?

18. The (personal / personnel) department will give you a (descent / decent) job if you apply.

19. Jerome (choose / chose) a new (pair / pear) of pants at the mall.

20. The (counsel / council) must approve the allocation before I give you the (lone / loan).

21. The restless kids tested my (patients / patience) as we waited for the (reign / rain / rein) to end.

22. In the meadow, the (flower / flour) swayed back and (forth / fourth) in the breeze.

23. I hope the bad (breaks / brakes) on the car do not (effect / affect) your driving.

24. The immense (wait / weight) of the (heard / herd) caused the truck to stall.

25. We studied (addition / edition) and subtraction during the (hole / whole) period.

Chapter Thirty Test A
Word Choice

Select the correct word(s) for each sentence.

1. After fifteen years with the same car, I _____ a new one.

a) have a need for

b) need

2. The dentist recommends that you brush your teeth _____.

a) daily

b) on a daily basis

3. At this _____, we aren't hiring new employees.

a) time

b) point in time

4. _____ that Santa was real.

a) He believed

b) Deep down inside he believed

5. We will move to our new house _____.

a) in the near future

b) soon

6. The centerpiece on the table was _____.

a) small

b) small in size

7. You need to _____ the rough draft and the final copy.

a) attach

b) attach together

8. _____, people commit more crimes than in the past.

a) In today's society

b) Today

9. Daniel sneezed _____ he was catching a cold.

a) due to the fact that

b) because

10. _____ that I deserved an apology from the rude waiter.

a) I felt

b) I felt inside

11. _____ I will be accepted into graduate school.

a) I think

b) In my mind, I think

12. _____ of us deserves a chance to go to college.

a) Each and every one

b) Each one

13. Filing the documents at the courthouse is a _____.

a) priority

b) top priority

14. Allow me to _____ to the events of last year.

a) refer back

b) refer

15. In my _____, I have never seen a specimen such as this.

a) past experience

b) experience

Chapter Thirty Test B
Word Choice
Rewrite the following sentences, removing general language, wordiness, and clichés.

1. Noah worked his fingers to the bone to save money for college.

2. At the wedding, I ate a lot of food.

3. Quality workmanship was sacrificed in order to meet the deadline.

4. I really needed a shoulder to cry on when Kayla jilted me at the altar.

5. In the bottom of his heart, Tyler sincerely felt he deserved the award.

6. Unable to make ends meet, I terminated my lease and went back to my parents' house.

7. The factory workers refuel the machines day in and day out.

8. Mix together the rice and the sauce before you serve them.

9. When she is late for work, Heather becomes a bad driver.

10. The faucet dripped for a long time before Madeline called a plumber.

11. The academic scholarships are awarded frequently.

12. In today's society, it is hard to know whom you can trust.

13. The graduates knew that hard work was required to climb the ladder of success.

14. Working in the summer heat without drinking fluids made me as sick as a dog.

15. In my personal opinion, I think the presentation was long and boring.

Chapter Thirty-One Test A

Sentence Variety

Identify the method used for sentence variety.

1. Dipped in batter, the chicken turned a golden brown in the skillet.

a) *ed* modifier

b) *ing* modifier

c) appositive

d) prepositional phrase

2. The trees that were supposed to be planted in the park ended up at the dump.

a) modifier

b) adverb

c) *who, which,* or *that* clause

d) appositive

3. My next door neighbor Mike Irving cuts his grass three times a week.

a) prepositional phrase

b) appositive

c) *ing* modifier

d) *ed* modifier

4. Hoping to get a ride to work, Sophia called all of her friends.

a) adverb

b) *ed* modifier

c) *who, which,* or *that* clause

d) *ing* modifier

5. Unfortunately, I lost my house keys.

a) prepositional phrase

b) *ed* modifier

c) appositive

d) adverb

6. Behind the tall woman was her frightened son.

a) prepositional phrase

b) appositive

c) *ing* modifier

d) *ed* modifier

7. Gary, who is also a teacher, is a brilliant lecturer.

a) *ed* modifier

b) adverb

c) *who*, *which*, or *that* clause

d) prepositional phrase

8. Monica gave me a compliment that made me smile.

a) adverb

b) *who*, *which*, or *that* clause

c) *ing* modifier

d) *ed* modifier

9. In the rear of the bus were several kids smoking cigarettes.

a) prepositional phrase

b) adverb

c) appositive

d) –ed modifier

10. Spooked by the strange noises, Amber ran out of the room.

a) -ing modifier

b) appositive

c) *who*, *which*, or *that* clause

d) adverb

11. Lovingly, the young woman looked into her boyfriend's eyes.

a) appositive

b) *ed* modifier

c) adverb

d) *ing* modifier

12. I have always loved the television show, <u>Survivor</u>.

a) prepositional phrase

b) appositive

c) *who*, *which*, or *that* clause

d) *ed* modifier

13. The crystal swan, sparkling in the sunlight, was an excellent centerpiece.

a) appositive

b) *ed* modifier

c) *ing* modifier

d) adverb

14. The car that Luis crashed could not be repaired.

a) *who*, *which*, or *that* clause

b) *ed* modifier

c) prepositional phrase

d) *ing* modifier

15. Around the corner ran the robber with a stolen television.

a) prepositional phrase

b) adverb

c) *ed* modifier

d) appositive

Chapter Thirty-One Test B
Sentence Variety

Combine the following pairs of sentences using the following: *-ing* modifiers; *-ed* modifiers; appositives; or *who, which,* or *that* clauses. Use each method at least once.

1. The parade began at seven o'clock.

   The parade celebrated Veteran's Day.

2. Samuel is the jury foreman.

   Samuel asked the irate juror to leave the room.

3. The talk show host interviewed guests.

   The host asked uninteresting questions.

4. The baby was wrapped in a fuzzy, pink blanket.

   The baby smiled and cooed.

5. The lion was exhausted after a successful hunt.

   The lion napped in the shade of a tree.

6. Plaza Theater is the only theater in town.

   It has only two screens.

7. The runner did not clear the last hurdle.
   He fell and sprained his wrist.

8. <u>Dark Knight</u> is the highest-rated show on the network.
   It airs on Thursday night at eight.

9. The teenager listened to the radio.
   The teenager danced to her favorite song.

10. The advertisement targeted senior citizens.
    The advertisement was filled with false promises.

194

CHAPTER TEST ANSWER KEY

Chapter One Test A

1. B
2. A
3. D
4. C
5. A
6. C
7. B
8. A
9. C
10. B
11. D
12. D
13. B
14. C
15. A

Chapter One Test B

1. A
2. B
3. N
4. OK
5. N
6. N
7. B
8. B
9. A
10. OK

11. Some guests do not bring gifts.
    The hostess is not always shown appreciation for her hard work.
12. a. T
    b. T
    c. TS
    d. T
    e. TS
13—15 . *Answers will vary.*:
    Ringing and buzzing of registers, holiday music, voices of shoppers, squealing children

Chapter Two Test A

1. B
2. A
3. C
4. D
5. B
6. D
7. A
8. D
9. C
10—15 *Answers will vary.*

Chapter Two Test B

1-20. *Answers will vary.*

Chapter Three Test A

1. A	9. D
2. C	10. A
3. D	11. C
4. B	12. A
5. A	13. D
6. B	14. B
7. A	15. C
8. C	

Chapter Three Test B

1. collector's items
2. rooms
3. *Answers will vary*:
   daisy, tulip, rose
4. *Answers will vary*:
   biker, boxer, basketball player
5. *Answers will vary*:
   Having a baby changes the atmosphere of a home.
6. Two infants slept in their cribs.
   A baby was crying.
7—9 . *Answers will vary.*
   Sweat glistened on her forehead.
   Her legs were shaking.
   She began to stammer.
10. time sequence

Chapter Four Test A

1. C	9. C
2. D	10. A
3. A	11. D
4. B	12. A
5. D	13. B
6. A	14. D
7. C	15. D
8. B	

Chapter Four Test B

1. b, c, f, h, j
2. Logan said, "Be careful when you cross the street."
3. "Don't talk with food in your mouth," Mom told us.
4. *Answers will vary:*
   Today at the park, Marco proved that violence is not the only way to handle conflicts.
5. Cathy served pizza and soda at the party.
   Several kids were dancing close to me.
   She was wearing a red-and-white dress.

Chapter Five Test A

1. C	9. B
2. A	10. C
3. B	11. D
4. D	12. A
5. C	13. B
6. B	14. C
7. D	15. B
8. A	

Chapter Five Test B

1. informational	11. OK	20. If I loosen my grip
2. directional	12. S	First, I comb out all of the tangles
3. OK	13. 2	I can't stop
4. B	14. 6	I part her hair in the middle
5. A	15. 4	Daria does not bother to thank me
6. S	16. 1	She just glares at me
7. OK	17. 7	
8. A	18. 5	
9. B	19. 3	
10. OK		

Chapter Six Test A

1. B	9. B
2. C	10. A
3. A	11. C
4. D	12. D
5. B	13. B
6. A	14. A
7. C	15. C
8. D	

Chapter Six Test B

1. to point out similarities
2. to point out differences

3—6 *Answers will vary.*

   3. We had to buy expensive camera equipment for the photography class; however, we needed only a calculator for the accounting class.

   4. Rick spends his entire vacation at the beach; similarly, Mike goes to the beach on weekends and each day after work.

5. Young girls swooned when they listened to songs by Elvis Presley in the '50s, and teenage girls fainted when Michael Jackson performed in the '90s.

6. The entertainment section of the newspaper gives a brief summary of current movies; on the other hand, movie critics on television discuss the actors, the plot, and the director in detail.

7—8. *Answers will vary.*

7. Army Basic Training and Marine Corps Boot Camp are similar in training, duration, and instructors.

8. Alligators and crocodiles differ in the appearance of the snout, the teeth, and the head.

9—10. point-by-point
subject-by-subject

Chapter Seven Test A

1. D	9. C
2. A	10. A
3. C	11. B
4. A	12. C
5. C	13. D
6. B	14. A
7. A	15. A
8. D	

Chapter Seven Test B

1. where it is placed in the house
2. type of monsters/creatures in it
3. how much the rooms cost

4—9. *Answers will vary.*

  4. toys for babies
  5. toys for toddlers
  6. toys for preteens
  7. overly helpful
  8. helpful
  9. do not help at all
  10. ballroom dancers
  11.ballet dancers
  12. disco dancers

13—15. *Answers will vary.*

Chapter Eight Test A

1. B	9. A
2. D	10. B
3. A	
4. C	
5. A	
6. D	
7. B	
8. C	

Chapter Eight Test B

1—3 . the term, the class or category, specific distinguishing characteristics

4—6. *Answers will vary*

  4. person, usually insecure and is cruel to smaller and weaker people

5. person, flaunts his or her supposed superiority over others or despises those who are considered inferiors

6. person, constantly tells of the deeds or plans of others

7—9. *Answers will vary*

10. A
11. C
12. A
13. A
14. C
15. C
16. A
17. A
18. C
19. A
20. C

Chapter Nine Test A

1. C	9. D
2. A	10. A
3. B	11. C
4. D	12. B
5. A	13. D
6. C	14. A
7. B	15. C
8. B	

Chapter Nine Test B

1. E
2. C
3. C
4. C
5. E
6. E
7. C
8. E
9. E
10. C

11—16 *Answers will vary*

11—13. get up earlier / must pack lunches / no time to eat breakfast

14—16. They don't study / They don't pay attention in class / They stay up too late.

17—18 *Answers will vary*

19. There were several reasons why Jessica quit her job.

20. My poor diet has negatively affected my health.

Chapter Ten Test A

1. A	9. B
2. C	10. A
3. B	11. C
4. D	12. D
5. B	13. B
6. C	14. A
7. A	15. C
8. D	

Chapter Ten Test B

1. S
2. OK
3. L
4. A
5. L
6. OK
7. S
8. A
9. S
10. OK
11. b
12. c
13. a , c
14. a, d
15. c
16. a

17—20. *Answers will vary.*

17—18 . Searches will uncover illegal drugs/guns.

   Stolen items can be recovered.

19—20. Vending machine food is less expensive than cafeteria food.

   Vending machines are convenient because of the quick service.

Chapter Eleven Test A

1. D	9. B
2. A	10. C
3. B	11. A
4. C	12. D
5. C	13. A
6. B	14. B
7. A	15. C
8. D	

Chapter Eleven Test B
1. N
2. OK
3. A
4. B
5. OK
6. A
7. B
8. OK
9. N
10. OK
11—15. *Answers will vary.*
11. Microwave meals are ideal because of the convenience, variety, and cost.
12. Universities and community colleges differ in cost, class sizes, and degree offerings.
13. People may have to use all of their money to make the payments.
    Creditors will constantly call the person at home and at work.
    Making late payments can cause the person to be denied credit at a later date.
1. She was not familiar with the inventory.
    She was rude to customers.
    She disregarded store policies.
2. It helps to gather information, contact school administrators, and visit the school when choosing a college to attend.

Chapter Twelve Test A

1. A	9. B
2. C	10. D
3. B	11. B
4. D	12. C
5. B	13. A
6. C	14. D
7. C	15. B
8. A	

Chapter Twelve Test B
Answers will vary.

Chapter Thirteen Test A

1. D	9. C
2. A	10. C
3. B	11. A
4. C	12. B
5. B	13. C
6. A	14. A
7. D	15. C
8. B	

Chapter Thirteen Test B

1—3. preread, read, reread with a pen or pencil
4. Treating what is read as half of a conversation and becoming involved
5—12. *Answers vary*
5—8. length, subheadings, charts, graphs, illustrations, underlined/italicized words, introductory material
9—12. mark main point, define words, question parts of the reading, react to the writer's ideas, add your own ideas, opinions, or examples
13—15. writer's main idea
   ideas used to explain the main idea
   examples used to support the main idea

Chapter Fourteen Test A

1. D	9. D
2. B	10. A
3. C	11. B
4. B	12. C
5. A	13. A
6. D	14. D

7—11. *Answers will vary.*
12. Ruben, S. Jordan. The Makers Diet. Lake Mary: Siloam, 2004.
13. Lazare, Aaron. "Go Ahead, Say You're Sorry." Psychology Today. Jan/Feb. 1995: 40—45 .
14. Malkin, Elisabeth. "Mexico Arrests Ex-Chief of Antidrug Agency." The New York Times 27 Nov. 2008: A6.
15. Chang, Hsiao-yun; Wallis, Marianne; Tiralongo, Evelin. "Use of complementary and alternative medicine among people living with diabetes: literature review." Journal of Advanced Nursing 58.4 (2007): 307—319.

Chapter Fifteen Test A

1. C	9. D
2. A	10. A
3. B	11. B
4. D	12. C
5. A	13. A
6. B	14. D
7. C	15. B
8. B	

Chapter Fifteen Test B

1. S-copies	V-are
2. S-shop, store	V-are
3. S-Juanita	V-is concerned
4. S-John, sister	V-will visit
5. S-puppy	V-chewed, swallowed
6. S-you	V-did attend

7. S-present	V-is
8. S-mayor	V-will approve
9. S-reasons	V-are
10. S-I	V-should have been considered
11. S-Biking	V-is
12. S-soup	V-tastes
13. S-Beverly	V-makes
14. S-turnout	V-is expected
15. S-Mike, Ted	V-wash
16. S-We	V-have studied
17. S-I	V-can hear
18. S-Flowers	V-are blooming
19. S-statue, bench	V-are
20. S-you	V-will attend

Chapter Sixteen Test A

1. D	9. C
2. A	10. D
3. B	11. A
4. C	12. B
5. A	13. C
6. D	14. B
7. B	15. D
8. B	

Chapter Sixteen Test B

1. *Answers will vary.*
2. *Answers will vary.*
3. *Answers will vary.*
4. *Answers will vary.*
5. *Answers will vary.*
6. *Answers will vary.*
7. rules, but
8. early; therefore,
9. educational; it
10. overhead; then
11. choice; nevertheless,
12. project; thus
13. table; all
14. box, and
15. parade; however,
16. dish; I
17. completely; therefore,
18. breakfast, nor
19. night, and
20. start, so

Chapter Seventeen Test A

1. D	9. D
2. C	10. A
3. B	11. C
4. B	12. C
5. A	13. B
6. C	14. B
7. D	15. D
8. B	

Chapter Seventeen Test B

Answers will vary.

Chapter Eighteen Test A

1. A	9. A
2. B	10. B
3. B	11. A
4. A	12. A
5. A	13. B
6. A	14. A
7. B	15. B
8. B	

Chapter Eighteen Test B

1—4. *Answers will vary.*
5. night, I
6. OK
7. raining, the
8. hours, I
9. OK
10. rings, both
11. OK
12. OK
13. adopted, my
14. OK
15. vacation, planning

Chapter Nineteen Test A

1. A	9. A
2. B	10. A
3. A	11. B
4. A	12. B
5. B	13. A
6. A	14. B
7. A	15. A
8. B	

Chapter Nineteen Test B

1. F	9. S
2. F	10. F
3. S	11. F
4. S	12. F
5. F	13. S
6. F	14. F
7. S	15. F
8. F	16-20: *Answers will vary.*

Chapter Twenty Test A

1. C	9. C
2. B	10. D
3. A	11. C
4. D	12. A
5. C	13. B
6. D	14. B
7. A	15. C
8. B	

Chapter Twenty Test B

1—10. *Answers will vary.*
11—14. *Answers will vary.*

Chapter Twenty-One Test A

1. D	9. A
2. B	10. D
3. A	11. A
4. D	12. B
5. C	13. C
6. B	14. A
7. A	15. D
8. B	

Chapter Twenty-One Test B

1. best	11. very, carefully
2. happy, lost	12. angrily
3. fur, bad	13. badly
4. Cold, winter	14. well
5. cautious, broken	15. rarely
6. large, green, dark	16. often
7. Dirty	17. barely
8. fat, little, blue, hungry	18. desperately
9. old, busy	19. slowly, cautiously
10. spoiled	20. successfully

III. When I was a young college student, I decided to major in English instead of biology. My decision was not made <u>quickly</u>. I knew that I had not done <u>well</u> in English in high school. I was a <u>better</u> biology student, so English was the <u>worse</u> choice. However, I did not choose <u>badly</u>. I studied hard and made <u>good</u> grades.

Chapter Twenty-Two Test A

1. B	9. A
2. C	10. C
3. A	11. D
4. D	12. A
5. B	13. C
6. A	14. B
7. C	15. A
8. B	

Chapter Twenty-Two Test B

Answers to sentences with modifier errors vary.
1. Weeding in her garden, Jenny stepped on a large snake.
2. We want to watch only cartoons on our television.
3. OK
4. My mother spent hours styling my tangled and dirty hair.
5. Running was difficult after I fell on the jogging path.
6. Smiling jubilantly, the winner returned to her chair.
7. As we were driving through the country, wildflowers scented the air.
8. OK
9. The clerk gave a sundae with a cherry on top to the child.
10. After the students spent six hours studying, the test was not difficult.
11. Because I was exhausted after working a double shift, the bed was warm and inviting.
12. Disturbed by the dancers, the lamp nearly tipped over.
13. Dressed in a new suit, Antonio was ready for the interview.
14. OK
15. We took the dog with fleas to the vet.

Chapter Twenty-Three Test A

1. D	9. D
2. B	10. B
3. C	11. B
4. A	12. C
5. D	13. D
6. C	14. A
7. C	15. B
8. A	

Chapter Twenty-Three Test B

1. contains	11. stands
2. was	12. doesn't
3. is	13. are
4. is	14. told
5. written	15. shines
6. have	16. listen
7. wants	17. walks
8. called	18. seen
9. made	19. tastes
10. does	20. told

Chapter Twenty-Four Test A

1. A	9. A
2. A	10. B
3. B	11. A
4. A	12. B
5. B	13. A
6. A	14. B
7. B	15. A
8. A	

Chapter Twenty-Four Test B

1. needs
2. eat
3. drinks
4. walk
5. is
6. flock
7. are
8. are
9. crosses
10. applies
11. takes
12. seems
13. do
14. hires
15. practice
16. matches
17. stay
18. receives
19. is
20. works

Chapter Twenty-Five Test A

1. A	9. A
2. B	10. B
3. B	11. B
4. A	12. B
5. B	13. B
6. A	14. A
7. B	15. B
8. B	

Chapter Twenty-Five Test B

1. her	11-20. *Answers will vary.*
2. his	
3. their	
4. their	
5. their	
6. its	
7. his	
8. his	
9. their	
10. its	

Chapter Twenty-Six Test A

1. A	9. B
2. B	10. B
3. A	11. A
4. A	12. A
5. B	13. B
6. A	14. B
7. A	15. A
8. B	

Chapter Twenty-Six Test B

1. he makes me pay
2. to exceed our budget
3. because he can catch
4. if they keep prices low
5. the caller always upsets me
6. since I get to meet
7. because she had to respect
8. we knew we would get
9. I/We could tell
10. tries to take advantage of me
11. me
12. me
13. we

14. I
15. him
16. she
17. its
18. they
19. I
20. us
21. me
22. us
23. he
24. me
25. she

Chapter Twenty-Seven Test A

1. C	9. C
2. B	10. D
3. A	11. A
4. A	12. B
5. D	13. B
6. B	14. A
7. A	15. B
8. B	

Chapter Twenty-Seven Test B

1. Mr. and Mrs. Smith asked their lawyer to prepare divorce papers.
2. Dr. Jackson received his M.D. last year.
3. Why did Ms. Williams leave church in the middle of service?
4. Miss Johnson is working on a B.A. in mathematics.
5. Did Mr. Chavez ask Mrs. Smith about volunteering at the fair?
6. Jack Pembroke, Jr., is nothing like his father, Jack Pembroke, Sr.
7. The 8 a.m. sessions at the gym have been postponed.
8. I went to work at 6 a.m.; I left at 5 p.m.
9. Mrs. Chung asked if Dr. Parker was teaching at the university in the fall.
10. The preacher married Mr. and Mrs. Walter Barker.

Chapter Twenty-Eight Test A

1. B
2. A
3. B
4. C
5. D
6. B
7. A
8. C
9. B
10. C

11. B
12. B
13. D
14. C
15. A

Chapter Twenty-Eight B

1. quitter
2. flies
3. beautiful
4. defensive
5. surely
6. shakier
7. churches
8. winning
9. potatoes
10. placement
11. height
12. fiend
13. believe
14. freight
15. perceive
16. Every time
17. anymore
18. Even though
19. downstairs
20. all ready
21. every one
22. high school
23. apart
24. bookkeeper
25. a lot

Chapter Twenty-Nine Test A

1. A
2. B
3. A
4. B
5. A
6. A
7. B
8. A
9. B
10. A
11. A
12. B
13. A
14. B
15. A

Chapter Twenty-Nine Test B

1. capital, farther
2. too, wait
3. You're, right
4. plane, site
5. quite, passed
6. steak, than
7. clothes, coarse
8. knew, fare
10. It's, hear
11. presents, patients
12. wined, through
13. aloud, altar
14. buy, cereal
15. moral, woman
16. Whether, we're
17. Would, dessert
18. personnel, decent
19. chose, pair
20. council, loan
21. patience, rain
22. flower, forth
23. brakes, affect
24. weight, herd
25. addition, whole

Chapter Thirty Test A

1. B	9. B
2. A	10. A
3. A	11. A
4. A	12. B
5. B	13. A
6. A	14. B
7. A	15. B
8. B	

Chapter Thirty Test B

1—15 *Answers will vary.*

1. Noah worked diligently to save money for college.
2. At the wedding, I ate two plates of food.
3. Quality workmanship was sacrificed to meet the deadline.
4. I really needed a friend when Kayla jilted me at the altar.
5. Tyler sincerely felt he deserved the award.
6. Unable to pay my bills, I terminated my lease and went back to my parents' house.
7. The factory workers refuel the machines daily.
8. Mix the rice and the sauce before you serve them.
9. When she is late for work, Heather becomes a reckless driver.
10. The faucet dripped for two days before Madeline called a plumber.
11. The academic scholarships are awarded once a month.
12. Today, it is hard to know whom you can trust.
13. The graduates knew that hard work was required to succeed.
14. Working in the summer heat without drinking fluids made me sick.
15. I think the presentation was long and boring.

Chapter Thirty-One Test A

1. A	9. A
2. C	10. D
3. B	11. C
4. D	12. B
5. D	13. D
6. A	14. A
7. C	15. A
8. B	

Chapter Thirty-One Test B

1—10. *Answers will vary.*